SCULTHORPE
SECRECY AND
STEALTH

SCULTHORPE
SECRECY AND STEALTH

A NORFOLK AIRFIELD IN THE COLD WAR

PETER B. GUNN

For Janet, Elspeth and all the family who have
given so much support and encouragement

Cover illustrations. Front: RB-45C 8034 of 19th Tactical Reconnaissance
Sqn, c. 1955. (David Whitaker) *Back:* The base from 1,500ft, August 1956.
(David Whitaker)

First published 2014

The History Press
The Mill, Brimscombe Port
Stroud, Gloucestershire, GL5 2QG
www.thehistorypress.co.uk

British Library Cataloguing in Publication Data.
A catalogue record for this book is available from the British Library.

ISBN 978 0 7524 7683 4

Typesetting and origination by The History Press
Printed in Great Britain

CONTENTS

GLOSSARY AND NOTE ON CURRENCY

AC1/AC2	Aircraftman 1st/2nd Class
AFB	Air Force Base
AFEX	Air Force Exchange *see* BX
AOC	Air Officer Commanding
BG	USAAF/USAF Bomb/Bombardment Group
BS	Bomb/Bombardment Squadron
BW	Bomb/Bombardment Wing
Butler sheds	Butler was an American company based in Kansas City that produced farm buildings. The US government had a contract with them and materials were shipped to Britain in kit form and assembled on site. Similar structures are to be found on many US airfields.
BX	Sometimes referred to as PX or AFEX. Base Exchange/Post Exchange. A department-style store on base similar to today's Wal-Mart.
CIA	Central Intelligence Agency
CO/OC	Commanding Officer/Officer Commanding
Commissary	The grocery store on base. Usually a military ID was necessary for purchases.
DFC	Distinguished Flying Cross
DSO	Distinguished Service Order
ECM	Electronic countermeasures
ELINT	Electronic Intelligence
FBW/FBS	Fighter-Bomber Wing/Fighter-Bomber Squadron
FFAF	Free French Air Force
FW/FS	Fighter Wing/Fighter Squadron
GCA	Ground Control Approach (radar)
GLCM	Ground launched cruise missile
Group	*see* Wing/Group
ICBM	Intercontinental Ballistic Missile

LABS	Low Altitude Bomb System
Marston sheds	The Marston type shed was introduced by the Air Ministry in 1943. It had an all-steel framework with walls of corrugated asbestos sheeting and a roof of corrugated steel sheeting.
MI5	The Security Service, commonly known as MI5 (Military Intelligence, Section 5) is the UK's internal counterintelligence and security agency and is part of its core intelligence machinery, alongside the Secret Intelligence Service (SIS or MI6) which is focused on foreign threats.
MOD	UK Ministry of Defence
NAAFI	Navy, Army and Air Force Institutes. The official trading organisation of HM Forces for providing retail and leisure services to the forces.
NATO	North Atlantic Treaty Organisation
NCO	Non-commissioned officer
Nissen huts	The Nissen hut was invented in 1915 by a Canadian Colonel, P.N. Nissen and the huts were manufactured from 1916. The design was widely used on airfields as a temporary building type and alternative to brick construction. The material used was corrugated iron and steel sheeting. The sizes varied from the 16ft span hut to the 24ft and 30ft span versions, to accommodate up to six bays, each bay of 6ft in width. Although designed to be temporary, many can still be seen today.
POL	Petroleum, Oil and Lubricants
PX	Post Exchange. A US Army term that survived the Air Force for years. *See* BX.
Quonset huts	US design of WW2 based on the British Nissen hut. The design was a lightweight prefabricated structure of corrugated galvanised steel having a semicircular cross section.
RAAF	Royal Australian Air Force
RNZAF	Royal New Zealand Air Force
SAC	US Air Force Strategic Air Command
SAM	Surface-to-air missile
SIGINT	Signals Intelligence
SRS/SRW	Strategic Reconnaissance Squadron/Wing
TAC	US Air Force Tactical Air Command
TACAN	Tactical Air Navigation System using a ground-based UHF transmitter providing bearing and distance information to the ground station from an aircraft.
TDY	Temporary duty, normally away from the home base, usually lasting for ninety days.

TFW	Tactical Fighter Wing
TRS/TRW	Tactical Reconnaissance Squadron/Wing
ULTRA	The name given to signals intelligence during the Second World War, obtained by breaking secret encrypted enemy communications. The work was carried out at the Government Code and Cypher School (GC&CS) at Bletchley Park.
USAFE	United States Air Forces in Europe
VHB	Very Heavy Bomber (airfield)
WAAF	Women's Auxiliary Air Force
Wing/Group	In the Second World War, the main unit of the US Army Air Force (USAAF) was the numbered group, either a fighter group (FG) or a bombardment group (BG). The group would form the basis of a combat wing, which would be placed within an air division. The group comprised a number of squadrons, usually three, and this would make up the fighting unit normally based at a particular station.

From September 1947, the United States Air Force was formed, independent of the Army, and the basic structure continued, except that the term 'group' gradually fell into disuse in favour of wing and was officially abandoned after 1951. Occasionally the wing acted as a headquarters unit based in the United States while the group (with the same identity number) was on overseas service. From the 1950s, the numbered wing became the main combat unit within the USAF, comprising three or four squadrons.

CURRENCY AND EXCHANGE RATES

Until decimal currency was introduced in Britain in 1971 amounts were stated in pounds, shillings, and pence. There were twelve pence in a shilling (12d) and twenty shillings in a pound (20s). Ten shillings became the equivalent of 50p in decimal currency, and the old shilling (1s) became 5p. Thus, predecimal currency is expressed in the book as (for example):

£1 2s 3d = One pound, two shillings and three pence.

The dollar/pound exchange rate was fixed between 1940 and 1971. The rate from 1949 until 1967 was $2.80 to the pound, and from 1967 until 1971 the rate was $2.40. After 1971 the value of the pound has effectively been allowed to float in value in foreign currency markets. In May 2013 the rate was approximately $1.50 to the pound.

INTRODUCTION AND ACKNOWLEDGEMENTS

There is much about Sculthorpe which has fascinated me since I lived at Harpley in the early 1980s, watching the American TR-1 spy planes (variant of the U-2) carrying out circuits and bumps, and the F111 bombers from Lakenheath, at the time that President Reagan was ordering the bombing raid against Colonel Gaddafi in Libya in April 1986. The airfield was in active use as a standby base but this was some years after its key role as a nuclear base at the height of the Cold War, which is the theme of this book.

April 2014 marks the sixtieth anniversary of the second secret flight over the Soviet Union from Sculthorpe by the Royal Air Force Special Duty Flight, one of the most intriguing operations in the early part of the Cold War and until recently one of the least known. There was much else that was clandestine about the history of the airfield and many unanswered questions about its role today. One fact is certain: the base has been central in the life of the local community for the best part of seventy years.

I have been very fortunate to have been able to contact some of those who recall the base in its heyday, both as servicemen and civilians. Many have been kind enough to lend me photographs and I have been endlessly entertained by their reminiscences and memories.

Barry Wells, Roger Lowe, Simon Thorpe, Tony Nelson, Verrall Grimes, Mr and Mrs John Odell and Gary Windeler have all provided valuable local knowledge. I have been exceptionally fortunate to receive help and advice from aviation historian Michael J.F. Bowyer, who generously supplied photographs and gave me permission to quote from his book *Force for Freedom*. Chris Lowe, a member of the Airfield Research Group, drew the three airfield plans included in the book. I am very grateful for copies of the photographs of the late Richard Jermy, who also provided much information about the airfield. Mike Hooks of *Aeroplane* magazine kindly sent me photographs of Sculthorpe-based aircraft. Flight Sergeant Mark Service, historian of the 67th Special Operations Squadron US Air Force (formerly the 67th Air Rescue Squadron), has been a valuable source of photographs and information. I have had several fascinating discussions with local historian Jim Baldwin about the airfield, which he has known since his boyhood. I would strongly recommend his pioneering works *40 Years of RAF Sculthorpe 1943–1983* (1986) and *RAF Sculthorpe: 50 Years of Watching and Waiting* (1999).

Thanks are also due to Roland Axman, Ted Barnes, Mrs K. Bygrave, Jenny Campling, Bob Collis and his colleague Kim Collinson, Mike Digby, Chris Doubleday, Mrs Joyce Doubleday, Eddie Piggott of the Green Park Centre at Sculthorpe, Allen Frary of the Wells Lifeboat Station, Graham Haynes, Cliff Howard, Donald Ketteringham, Muriel Kidd, Avril MacArthur, John Maiden, Anne Manning (née Teviotdale), R.T. Newman, Steve Nowell, Linda Nudds, Peter Pells, Sheena Riches, Steve Snelling, Bob Vigar, the late Wing Commander Ken Wallis MBE, Jim Wheeler, Allan Womack and Robin Woolven.

Many American veterans and their families generously supplied information and photographs via letters, Facebook, email and various websites. I am very grateful for the help of Donald Aspinall, Dr Robert Boudreau, Bill Blythe, Misha ben-David, Dan and Jan Daley, Nathan Decker and his website *Forgotten Jets*, Donald Hall, Herbert Kulik, Kathy Leming, Joan Sheppard Lio, John Lucero, Lou Natale, John Northcut, Jerry Paradis, Janet Duwe Ramsey, Jerry Roth, Karen Bell Ruskin, Allen Shockley, Jewel M. 'Nip' Smart, Bill and Jean Tollefson, Jerry Wickstrum and David S. Whitaker. Some of these contacts have been made possible through the Sculthorpe group site on Facebook, which remains a constant source of information and entertainment about life at the base over the years.

In the course of my research I consulted many archives and sources, all cited in the text and bibliography. These include the National Archives at Kew, British Library Newspapers at Colindale, the Royal Air Force Museum library at Hendon, Cambridge University Library, the Royal Air Force Historical Society, and the online resource of the Air Force Historical Research Agency at Maxwell Air Force Base. Local sources have included the Fakenham Museum of Gas and Local History, the Norfolk Record Office, Norfolk Heritage Centre and the Norfolk Historic Environment Record of Norfolk County Council, the 2nd Air Division (USAAF) Memorial Library in Norwich and the Norfolk and Suffolk Aviation Museum at Flixton near Diss.

My thanks are also due to the staff of the Stanford Training Area (STANTA) based in Thetford, who have given up their time on several occasions to escort me around the Ministry of Defence section of airfield site.

I am very grateful to the editors at The History Press, in particular Chrissy McMorris, who supervised the production of this book. My sister Elspeth Mackinlay once again took on the tedious but vital task of proofreading and saved me from many errors. My wife Janet has always been a source of encouragement and support in the long and laborious process of research and writing, in spite of my neglect of many household tasks.

COPYRIGHT PERMISSIONS

Extracts and photographs cited in textual notes and the bibliography are reproduced by kind permission of several publishers and authors. These include Paul Lashmar, author of *Spy Flights of the Cold War* (Sutton Publishing 1996), and Bruce Williamson from the website www.spyflight.co.uk.

Extracts from the books of Colonel Wolfgang W.E. Samuel (USAF, retired) are reproduced by permission of the author and Cynthia Foster, Permissions Manager of the University Press of Mississippi (see bibliography and footnotes for details). Extracts from *The B-45 Tornado: An Operational History of the First American Jet Bomber* by John C. Fredriksen (2009) are reproduced by kind permission of Lois Grubb, Business Manager, McFarland & Company, Inc., Jefferson NC.

Extracts from newspapers are reproduced by permission of Solo Syndication (the *Daily Mail*, a division of Associated Newspapers UK Ltd), Mirrorpix (the *Daily Mirror*), *The Star* (Sheffield Newspapers Limited, editor Jeremy Clifford), and the *Lynn News* (editor Nick Woodhead and photographer Paul Tibbs).

Wing Commander C.G. Jefford gave me permission to quote from 'Air Intelligence: A Symposium', *Journal of the Royal Air Force Historical Society*, in Chapter Eight (Secret Flights).

Every effort has been made to contact copyright holders but if there are any errors or omissions, I would be glad to rectify these in future editions.

Peter B. Gunn,
Docking, Norfolk, September 2013.

TIMELINES

	Norfolk & Regional	National & International
1942	*29–30 Apr.* First 'Baedeker' raid on Norwich, part of a campaign in 1942 and 1943 to bomb some of the historic cities of England, including Ipswich, Bath, Exeter and King's Lynn. Bombing campaign from East Anglian airfields. USAAF begins to arrive in England. Shipdham becomes first USAAF heavy bomber base in Norfolk. Operational from October. Sculthorpe airfield built by Bovis Ltd and Constable Hart Ltd towards end of year.	*Sep.* Manhattan Project begins in USA to design and build an atomic bomb. *Oct.–Nov.* Battle of El Alamein – turning point for Allies in North Africa.
1943	*Jan.* Mosquitoes from RAF Marham carry out the first daylight raid on Berlin. *May* No. 342 'Lorraine' Sqn first unit to arrive at Sculthorpe. Station ceases to be satellite. *Jun.* 2 Gp RAF assigned to newly formed 2nd Tactical Air Force with HQ at Bylaugh Hall, Dereham. *Jul.–Sep.* Mosquitoes of Nos. 464, 487 and 21 Sqns arrive and train for invasion support. Sculthorpe designated No. 140 Airfield. Sculthorpe opens as satellite for W. Raynham within No. 2 Gp RAF.	*Jan.* German surrender at Stalingrad. *Feb.–May* Rommel in full retreat in Tunisia. End of German and Italian resistance in N. Africa. *May* 617 Sqn 'Dam Busters' raid. Tide turns against U-Boats in Atlantic. *Jul.* Germans defeated by Soviets at Kursk. Allied invasion of Sicily. Mussolini falls from power in Italy. *Sep.* Allied landings at Messina and Salerno.

Norfolk & Regional	National & International
32 Horsa gliders arrive for storage. Sculthorpe ceases to be a satellite and becomes a station in its own right. *Nov.* No. 100 (Bomber Support) Gp RAF formed – for radio countermeasures (RCM). *Dec.* No. 140 Wing squadrons leave Sculthorpe for Hunsdon as No. 2 Gp squadrons move south.	Italy signs armistice.

| **1944** | *Jan.–Jun.*
100 Gp HQ moves to Bylaugh Hall, Dereham.

Jan.
First units of 100 Gp RAF arrive at Sculthorpe (214 Sqn RAF and 803rd Bomb Sqn (BS) USAAF.

May
Sculthorpe closes for conversion into a Very Heavy Bomber (VHB) Airfield. | *Jan.*
Allied landings at Anzio.
Soviet forces break siege at Leningrad.

Steady advance drives Germans back.

May
Allies break German resistance at Monte Cassino – turning point in Italy.

6 Jun.
D-Day landings in Normandy.

V1 flying bomb campaign begins.

Sep.
V2 Rocket campaign against London and East Anglia.

Battle of Arnhem.

Dec.
German counterattack in Ardennes – 'Battle of the Bulge'. |
| **1945** | *8 May*
Victory in Europe Day – VE Day

15 Aug.
Victory over Japan – VJ Day | *Feb.*
Dresden bombed.

Mar.
Allies cross Rhine.

May
Germany surrenders.

Jul.
US explodes world's first atomic bomb in New Mexico. |

	Norfolk & Regional	National & International
		Aug. Japanese surrender follows A–bombs on Hiroshima and Nagasaki.
1946	*Mar.* Visit of Boeing B–29A Superfortresses to Marham for joint Anglo-US bomb trials lasting 180 days in Operation 'Ruby'.	*Mar.* Churchill's speech at Fulton, Missouri, USA: 'An iron curtain has descended across the continent.' The US Army Air Force creates three new combat commands: Strategic Air Command (SAC), Air Defense Command (ADC) and Tactical Air Command (TAC). *Aug.* US Congress passes the McMahon Act (Atomic Energy Act) which prohibits supply of information on atomic matters to any other nation.
1947	*Jun.* First deployment of USAAF B–29 bombers to England, from 340th Bomb Sqn (BS), arriving Marham 9 June, for one week. This is the first American deployment of bombers to the UK since the end of the Second World War.	*Sep.* US Air Force becomes an independent service. Boeing B–50 bomber (upgraded and modified version of the B–29) begins to replace the B–29 in SAC during year.
1948	*Aug.* In response to the international situation the US 3rd Air Div. (Provisional) sets up HQ at Marham. For the first time, US forces were being stationed in a friendly country in peacetime. USAF B–29 Bomb Groups are despatched in rotation for 90-day periods (TDYs) to various East Anglian bases, the 28th Bomb Gp (BG) to Scampton, the 307th BG to Marham with the 372nd Bomb Sqn (BS) to Waddington, and the 2nd BG to Lakenheath.	*Apr.* US President Harry S. Truman announces Marshall Plan – offering economic aid to west European nations. *Jun.* Berlin crisis. Soviets blockade all land routes to city and Allies begin airlift, named Operation 'Vittles'. *Sep.* 3rd Air Div. HQ moves to Bushy Park nr London. *Oct.* Lt Gen. Curtis LeMay takes command of USAF Strategic Air Command (SAC).
1949	Sculthorpe reopens as Very Heavy Bomber (VHB) Airfield.	*Apr.* 3rd Air Div. HQ moves to South Ruislip.

Norfolk & Regional	National & International
Feb. 92nd BG of USAF SAC becomes first unit to arrive. B-29 bombers on TDY to counter Soviet threats over Berlin. This was part of the 3rd TDY UK deployment. SAC units continue to use airfield on 90-day rotation. *Aug.* B-50A *Lucky Lady II* 46-010 arrives at airfield (63rd BS, 43rd BG). (Feb. to March covered 23,452 miles in first round-the-world non-stop flight.) *18 Nov.* Crew flying a Douglas C-74 Globemaster I *The Champ* lands at RAF Marham after a 23-hour flight from Mobile, Alabama, USA. On board are a transatlantic-record 103 passengers and crew.	*May* Berlin blockade lifted. Tension remains high. North Atlantic Treaty signed. NATO formed. *Jul.* USSR explodes first atomic bomb. *Sept.* Federal Republic of Germany (West Germany) founded. *Oct.* Communist People's Republic of China founded under Mao. German Democratic Republic (East Germany) founded.
1950 *Mar.* First of 4 B-29 Superfortresses (named Washingtons) supplied to RAF. First equip No. 149 Sqn at Marham. Lakenheath declared the US base in UK with the best potential – runways 1 x 9,000ft, 2 x 6,000ft.	*Jan.* Mutual Defence Assistance Agreement signed with USA under the North Atlantic Treaty. B-29 bombers to be delivered to RAF. *Jun.* Korean War begins. North Korea invades South Korea. A diversionary attack by the Soviets in Western Europe is feared. Plans to increase USAF deployments in UK.
1951 *Jan.* USAF formally takes over Sculthorpe as tenant. Arrival of North American RB-45C at Sculthorpe with the 91st Strategic Reconnaissance Wing (SRW) – the first operational four-jet aircraft. *Jul.* Three Convair B-36 bombers overfly *Festival of Britain* London Exhibition on way to Paris Air Show.	*Mar.* USAF Strategic Air Command (SAC) 7th Air Div. HQ at South Ruislip nr London to take charge of all SAC bomber and fighter units visiting UK on rotation. *May* USAF 3rd Air Div. becomes Third Air Force, HQ South Ruislip. Tactical units now added to Third AF responsibilities based at Mildenhall, Lakenheath, Sculthorpe, Wyton and Bassingbourn, and fighter jets at Manston, Kent.

Norfolk & Regional	National & International
Nov. B-36 bombers arrive on detachment for the first time to Sculthorpe.	First British RAF jet bomber, Canberra, in RAF service – 101 Sqn (May 1951).
12–18 Dec. Visual Bombing Competition Joint Winners 9th Bomb Wing (BW) and 301st Bomb Wing (BW) (B-29s).	First flight of Vickers Valiant prototype – to become first of RAF V-bomber force. *Oct.* Winston Churchill returns as prime minister. US 49th Air Div. activated to supervise and control USAF operations.
1952 *17–18 Apr.* First of the 'secret flights' over the USSR by the RAF Special Duty Flt from Sculthorpe. *May–Jun.* US 49th Air Div. HQ moves to Sculthorpe (until July 1956). Component parts the 47th Bomb Wing (BW) (at Sculthorpe) and 20th Fighter-Bomber Wing (FBW) based at Wethersfield, Essex, and Woodbridge, Suffolk.	*6 Feb.* Death of King George VI at Sandringham. *Oct.* First British atomic bomb exploded at Monte Bello, Australia. *Nov.* US explodes first hydrogen bomb. Dwight D. Eisenhower elected US President.
1953 *Jan.–Feb.* East coast floods. Damage and loss of life. Sculthorpe personnel assist in the crisis.	*Mar.* Soviet leader Joseph Stalin dies. Nikita Khrushchev succeeds. *Jun.* Queen Elizabeth II crowned. *Jul.* Korean War armistice signed. *Aug.* USSR explodes first hydrogen bomb. *Nov.* First RAF atomic bomb 'Blue Danube' into service.
1954 *28–29 Apr.* 'Secret flight' over USSR by RAF Special Duty Flt from Sculthorpe. By the middle of the year tactical nuclear weapons were being stored here by the USAF here. *May* Sculthorpe hosts first 'open day'.	*Mar.* US tests hydrogen bomb.

Norfolk & Regional	National & International
Dec. *Daily Mail* articles reveal Sculthorpe as a nuclear base for the first time.	

	Norfolk & Regional	National & International
1955	Alconbury becomes a satellite airfield of Sculthorpe until the end of the year, when it becomes an independent station of the Third Air Force. *29 Mar.* 3 USAF RB-45C Tornados of 19th Tactical Reconn. Sqn (TRS) make secret flight over USSR military installations and cities. Soviet fighters were scrambled but unable to locate the US aircraft at night. All three aircraft return safely to their base in West Germany.	*Feb.* First RAF V-bomber, the Valiant, into service. *May* West Germany becomes member of NATO. Rearmament follows. *Bundeswehr* (Armed Forces of Federal German Republic – West Germany) formed. Warsaw Pact (USSR and Allies) formed. *Jun.* Boeing B-52 enters service with USAF. *Jul.* First of the 4-Power Summits held at Geneva to open up dialogue and reduce tension in Cold War: US, Britain, USSR and France. Eisenhower had approved secret flight (of 29 March) to gain up-to-date intelligence beforehand.
1956	*15 Mar.* Arrival of the first Valiant V-bomber to 214 Sqn at Marham. *Apr.* Soviet leaders Khrushchev and Bulganin visit Marham during their visit to the UK. *Jul.* 49th Air Div. disbanded at Sculthorpe.	*May* Vulcan enters service with RAF. *Oct.* Hungarian uprising against USSR. *Nov.* Suez crisis.
1957	*Feb.* Douglas RB-66 Destroyers begin to replace the RB-45s in the 19th TRS at Sculthorpe.	*Aug.* First Soviet Intercontinental Ballistic Missile (ICBM) launched. *Oct.* Soviet *Sputnik* launched (world's first artificial satellite). *Nov.* Victor V-bomber enters RAF service. Britain's Operation 'Grapple' – first UK hydrogen bomb exploded.

	Norfolk & Regional	National & International
		Dec. US launch Atlas missile – first American ICBM.
1958	*Jan.* Douglas B-66B Destroyers begin to replace the B-45s in the 47th BW at Sculthorpe. *Sep.* Feltwell becomes first HQ base for US-built Thor ballistic missiles (ICBMs). 4 satellite bases included Mepal, North Pickenham, Shepherds Grove and Tuddenham. Eventually there would be 20 Thor launch sites in East Anglia and Yorkshire.	*Jan.* Campaign for Nuclear Disarmament (CND) formed.
1959	Thor deployments (as above).	*Jan.* Fidel Castro comes to power in Cuba. *Feb.* US launch first Titan ICBM. *Jun.* First ballistic missile-carrying US submarine launched – USS *George Washington*. Summer – Gen. Charles de Gaulle orders all US nuclear weapons out of France. USAF units redistributed to W. Germany, England and USA.
1960	48th Tactical Fighter Wing (TFW) moves from France to Lakenheath.	*Feb.* First French atom bomb test. France becomes fourth nuclear power. *May* US pilot Gary Powers shot down in U-2 spy plane over USSR.
1961		*Jan.* John F. Kennedy becomes US President. *Apr.* Yuri Gagarin of USSR becomes first man in space. 'Bay of Pigs' attempted invasion of Cuba.

	Norfolk & Regional	National & International
		May Alan Shepard becomes first US man in space. *Aug.* Berlin Wall erected by USSR.
1962	*Jun.* 47th BW deactivated at Sculthorpe and airfield becomes a standby base. 7375th Support Group to administer base until 1964.	*Oct.* Cuban missile crisis.
1963	*Aug.* Phase-out of Thor missiles completed.	*Jan.* Britain announces building of nuclear powered ballistic missile submarines and purchase of US Polaris missiles. *Aug.* UK, USA and USSR sign limited Test Ban Treaty to end atmospheric nuclear testing. *Nov.* President Kennedy assassinated.
1964	*Mar.* 420th Air Refuelling Squadron leaves Sculthorpe for Edwards AFB. *The last permanent flying unit at the base.* Sculthorpe returns to RAF use.	*Oct.* Khrushchev ousted from power in Soviet Union. China detonates first nuclear weapon.
1965		*Mar.* US marines deploy to Vietnam. US start to bomb N. Vietnam. *Apr.* TSR2 aircraft cancelled.
1966		*Mar.* Gen. de Gaulle announces that France will withdraw from NATO by 1967. US forces given notice to withdraw from France.
1967	*Jan.* USAF Stores Depot reopens at Sculthorpe as result of USAF withdrawal from France. No plans to station aircraft at present.	*Jun.* Arab–Israeli Six-Day War. China explodes first hydrogen bomb.

	Norfolk & Regional	National & International
	Apr. Sculthorpe becomes a Standby Dispersal Base for the 48th Tactical Fighter Wing (TFW) based at Lakenheath. 7519th Combat Support Sqn to administer base.	*Aug.* France explodes hydrogen bomb.
1968	Sculthorpe's main runway resurfaced. Some demolition of buildings and refurbishment of existing buildings.	*Jun.* First Polaris submarine into service. *Aug.* Soviet forces crush Czech 'Prague Spring'.
1969		*Jun.* 'Strategic quick reaction' passes from RAF to RN Polaris submarines. *Jul.* Apollo 11 lands on moon – first manned moon landing.
1970		*Mar.* Nuclear non-Proliferation Treaty ratified by US, UK and USSR.
1971		
1972	*Apr.* US Third Air Force HQ moves to Mildenhall. *Sep.* First *Flintlock* exercise (*Flintlock V*) at Sculthorpe.	*May* SALT I Strategic Arms Limitation Agreement signed.
1973		*Jan.* Britain joins European Union. Vietnam Peace Treaty. *Oct.* Yom Kippur War and oil crisis.
1974		*Mar.* First flight of RAF Tornado prototype.
1975		*Apr.* US pulls out of Vietnam
1976	7519th CSS disbanded. Sculthorpe handed back to MOD. Base now Detachment 1 of the 48th TFW.	*Sep.* Chinese Chairman Mao Tse-Tung dies.

	Norfolk & Regional	National & International
1977	Runways resurfaced. Base used for exercises.	Soviet SS-20 missiles deployed in Europe.
1978	*Jul.* First RAF aircraft return to Sculthorpe: Victor K2 Tankers from Nos. 55 and 57 Sqns, RAF Marham.	
1979		*Dec.* NATO deploys 572 Pershing missiles and ground launched cruise missiles (GLCMs). USSR invades Afghanistan.
1980		*Jul.* Britain announces purchase of US Trident system.
1981	MAP Project (Mutual Military Assistance Program) at Sculthorpe. Danish and Norwegian Air Forces fly in surplus North American F-100s, Lockheed Starfighters and T-33s for conversion to Turkish Air Force. Also ex-French Air Force aircraft arrive for scrapping.	
1982		*Apr.–Jun.* Falklands War. *Jun.* Tornado enters service with RAF.
1983		*Mar.* President Reagan announces Strategic Defense Initiative (SDI) – 'Star Wars'. *Nov.* First cruise missiles arrive at RAF Greenham Common.
1984	CND starts 'Snowball' campaign, demonstrating at a number of US bases including Sculthorpe. Symbolic wire cutting of perimeter fencing. Arrests made.	
1985	'Snowball' campaign continues in spring.	*Mar.* Mikhail Gorbachev becomes Soviet leader.

	Norfolk & Regional	National & International
1986	*15–16 Apr.* US 48th TFW based at Lakenheath take part in raid on Libya.	*Apr.* Operation 'Eldorado Canyon' – US attack on suspected terrorist targets in Libya.
1987		*Dec.* US and USSR sign Intermediate Nuclear Forces Treaty – Pershings, GLCMs and Warsaw Pact SS-20s to be withdrawn from Europe.
1988		*Apr.* Last Lightning fighter withdrawn from RAF.
1989		*Year of collapse of Soviet power in Eastern Europe.* *Nov.* Berlin Wall taken down.
1990		*Aug.* Iraq invades Kuwait. *Oct.* Germany unified.
1991	Sculthorpe tasked with supplying Medivac role. Not required in the end.	*Jan.* First Gulf War – Operation 'Desert Storm'. *May* GLCM wing (cruise missiles) deactivated at Greenham Common. *Jul.* Warsaw Pact dissolved. *Sep.* Royal Observer Corps disbanded. *Dec.* USSR dissolved.
1992	*2 Oct.* US Air Force finally departs from Sculthorpe. Base handed over to MOD.	

1. BEGINNINGS

RAF West Raynham in Norfolk had opened in April 1939 as a grass field, and with the start of the war in September began to operate within No. 2 Group Bomber Command. By July 1940, a satellite airfield had been established 2½ miles to the east at Great Massingham.

By 1942 an enormous expansion of the air war was taking place, with the RAF bomber offensive against Germany building up and the anticipated arrival of units from the United States Army Air Force (USAAF). The Air Ministry had an insatiable requirement for further airfield building and East Anglia was in the front line of the expanding air war. Existing airfields were developed with concrete runways, and new sites were found to act as satellite airfields.

Concrete runways were being laid at West Raynham during 1942 (and soon at Great Massingham) and a second satellite airfield was planned at a site 4 miles to the north. The airfield at Sculthorpe took its name from the small village to its east. The place name originates from an Old Norse personal name, Skúli, + thorp, an 'outlying settlement' or 'hamlet'. The village was mentioned in the Domesday Book as having 60 acres of glebe land. As airfields were usually named after the parish in which they were situated, the site found itself straddled between the parishes of Dunton and Tattersett, which were actually nearer to what became the airfield than the village of Sculthorpe. Close by, just to the north-west, lay the village of Syderstone.

Work began in the spring of 1942 and the airfield was laid out as a standard RAF Class A bomber airfield with concrete runways, dispersals, mess facilities and accommodation. Brazen Hall Farmhouse, which stood at the planned centre of the airfield, had to be demolished.

Much of the work was completed by Irish labour. Local residents Peter Pells and Muriel Kidd recalled the bulldozers moving in during 1942 and the arrival of Irish labourers, who had to live in tents in the area which later became Blenheim Park. The labourers did not seem to venture much outside the camp because the work went on day and night and they had their own bars and facilities, although at least one Irishman was known to have married a local girl.

The airfield construction was to involve the closure of two country roads (see Chapter Three). The runway lengths were 2,000 yards and 1,400 yards for the two subsidiaries. The usual thirty-six hardstandings were provided, all loops, while the technical area with two T2 hangars lay on the west side of the airfield, with two communal and seven domestic dispersed sites, for 1,773 males and 409 females further to the west. There were two more T2 hangars. Bomb stores were situated on the south of the technical site. The contractors were John Laing, Bovis Ltd and Constable Hart & Co. Ltd, which had completed the station by October 1943.

In May 1943, the station ceased to be a satellite of West Raynham and became an independent RAF station, ready to receive the first units.

2. FIRST UNITS (1943–44)

> 'Sculthorpe was a bleak, windswept collection of Nissen huts, very unlike the cosy permanent buildings of Swanton.'
>
> **(Arthur Eyton-Jones, No. 21 Squadron, 1943)**

By 1943, Allied planning for Operation 'Overlord', the invasion of Europe, began to filter down to individual airfields and units. In common with many airfields in the eastern counties, space had to made available at Sculthorpe for the storage of thirty-two Horsa gliders from February 1943 until March of the following year.

Another aspect of strategic planning was the reorganisation of RAF Bomber Command. West Raynham, and now Sculthorpe, came within the ambit of No. 2 Bomber Group, equipped with light bombers, but on 1 June 1943 the group was assigned to the newly formed Second Tactical Air Force as part of the preparations for the invasion of Europe and the support of the forces in the field. The group was commanded by the legendary air commander Air Vice-Marshal Basil Embry who, from his headquarters at Bylaugh Hall near Dereham, began the uphill task of welding his motley collection of squadrons and crews into an effective fighting force.

NO. 342 (LORRAINE) SQUADRON (FFAF)

The first flying unit to arrive at Sculthorpe was No. 342 (Lorraine) Squadron, Free French Air Force (FFAF). The squadron had originated in Damascus in Syria as The Lorraine Squadron during September 1941. After service in the Middle East campaign the personnel were posted to England and the squadron reformed at West Raynham on 7 April 1943 with the motto 'Nous y sommes' ('Here we are'). With their Douglas Boston Mark IIIA bombers the Frenchmen moved to Sculthorpe on 15 May organised in two flights, 'A' or Metz Flight and 'B' or Nancy Flight, under the command of Lieutenant Colonel Henri de Rancourt.

No. 342 (Lorraine) Squadron badge. The first flying unit at Sculthorpe. Motto *'Nous y sommes'* – 'Here we are'.

Many of the personnel of the squadron were to become household names after the war. They included Pierre Mendès France who, like many of his countrymen, had escaped from Vichy France to take up arms with General Charles de Gaulle's Free French Forces. He was eventually to become French Prime Minister from 1954–55. Possibly better known was Bernard Citroën, the eldest son of André Citroën, founder of the car company of that name. Bernard became a pilot in the squadron during 1944, after the unit had left Sculthorpe. His fame rests on his distinguished war record and his prominence as a poet and writer in later years.

The short period spent at Sculthorpe was taken up mainly by training, for example, in bombing exercises at the Grimston Warren range, but this did not leave the squadron unscathed. On 22 May, all four of the crew of Boston AL285 were killed in a crash at low-level near Rougham. They included Lieutenant Le Bivic (pilot), Observer Sous-Lieutenant Jacouinot, Sergent-Chef L. Cohen and Caporal-Chef Desertiaux.

On 12 June, the squadron mounted its first operation when three aircraft, along with nine from 107 Squadron, were detailed to attack Rouen power station. Shortly after this, one aircraft from a formation of three failed to return from a low-level raid to Langerbrugge in Belgium: Boston BZ366 with Sous-Lieutenant Pineau (pilot) and crew.

The French National Day parade on 14 July (Bastille Day) at Sculthorpe had to be cancelled due to a squadron standby for a diversionary raid on Abbeville aerodrome. Six aircraft from the squadron accompanied twelve from 107 Squadron in what appears to have been a successful attack. Later that day Lieutenant Colonel Rancourt was able to host a dinner and dance by way of celebration. The stay at Sculthorpe was nearly over, for on 19 July the order came through for the squadron to move to nearby Great Massingham.

NOS. 487 (RNZAF), 464 (RAAF) AND 21 SQUADRONS – NO. 140 WING

Basil Embry, AOC 2 Group, had been lobbying hard to obtain Mosquito Mark VI fighter-bombers (FBVIs) to replace the Lockheed Venturas, Douglas Bostons and North American Mitchells in his squadrons. On 20 and 21 July 1943, Nos 464 and

Left–right: No. 487 Squadron (RNZAF) badge. Motto '*Ki te mutunga*' – 'Through to the end';
No. 464 Squadron (RAAF) badge. Motto '*Aequo animo*' – 'Equanimity'; No. 21 Squadron
badge. Motto '*Viribus vincimus*' – 'By strength we conquer'. Squadron was reformed at nearby
Bircham Newton in December 1935. In the Second World War the squadron was unofficially
named 'Norwich's own squadron'.

487 Squadrons moved from Methwold to Sculthorpe with their Venturas, eager
to begin conversion to the new type and abandon their 'pigs', as they called them.
The problem with the Ventura was that it proved far too slow and vulnerable for daylight operations while the Mosquito was more than proving its worth, for example
in the daylight raids on Berlin from nearby Marham on 30 January. Embry had been
anxious to move his newly formed 140 Wing to a base further south nearer to the
invasion targets, but with no suitable airfields available at the time and Sculthorpe
now vacant due to the French move, Sculthorpe it had to be.

Embry was anything but an armchair commander and he was keen to appoint
a like-minded individual to command the Wing, whom he found in the person of
Group Captain Percy C. 'Pick' Pickard DSO, DFC. Pickard, at the age of 28, already
had an outstanding operational record behind him as the Wellington pilot 'star' in the
1940 RAF propaganda film *Target for Tonight*. He had received a bar to his DSO for his
part in transporting the commandos in the Bruneval raid of February 1942, and a
second bar for clandestine work from RAF Tempsford conveying secret agents of the
Special Operations Executive (SOE) to France. He was about to be posted to a non-
operational post but made use of his network of contacts to have this changed to the
command of No. 140 Wing towards the end of July.

Pickard wasted no time in making his presence felt at Sculthorpe although the
surroundings left much to be desired. Mike Henry, a wireless operator/air gunner
with 487 Squadron and newly arrived from Methwold, recalled entering the Nissen
hut which was the Officers' Mess and making for the bar. Standing by it was the new

Wing Commander Percy 'Pick' Pickard as CO of No. 161 Squadron at Tempsford, with Lysander in background. 'Ming', the old English sheepdog, in foreground left.

station commander Group Captain Pickard with his grizzled old sheepdog, Ming. Pickard watched in silent amusement as he ordered three large bitters. It turned out that there was no bitter, Scotch or gin. This seemed to confirm Mike's first impressions of the camp: empty and uninteresting.

The group captain butted in at that stage: 'I'm afraid that we have caught the staff unawares. The Free French left here a few days ago and left us nothing but a hogshead of red biddy. We'll have to make the best of it until supplies arrive.'

The best on offer turned out to be potions of undrinkable cheap wine and Mike Henry 'spent the rest of the evening trying to untie my tongue'. A bar with no beer was hardly a good start to the posting.[1]

Another drawback was that the Mosquito had a crew of two, pilot and navigator, and not four as in the Ventura, so it was farewell to a few dozen wireless operators and air gunners who had been with the squadrons for some time. By early August, the training programme was starting in earnest, with physical training and unarmed combat for the crews. Then the first Mosquitoes began to arrive from the de Havilland factory in Hatfield and the serious conversion began. There was general delight with the new aircraft – the squadrons were as pleased as children with a new toy, but Pickard worked them hard and hated to see a Mosquito on the ground. After a very hot July with some thundery weather, there was constant cold wind and rain towards the end of August which made life more difficult for the ground crews who had only one hangar on the airfield to maintain the aircraft. The rest of the work had to be done in the open dispersal areas, across roads and into wheat fields. The problems got worse in what turned out to be a very cold winter, the first signs of which appeared in early November.

On 27 September the third squadron, No. 21, had moved in and the Wing was now complete and ready for operations. The personnel of the squadrons included Australians, New Zealanders, Canadians, a Frenchman, a South African and four Americans who had joined the Canadian Air Force before the United States declared war (and consequently lost their American citizenship). The remainder included a good sprinkling of Scots, Welsh and Irish, many from neutral Southern Ireland.[2]

A newcomer to 21 Squadron in October was Arthur Eyton-Jones, freshly posted from Swanton Morley where he had been a navigator on B-25 Mitchells with 226 Squadron. He had already survived being shot down off the Dutch coast and spending six days in a dinghy awaiting rescue after his aircraft was attacked by German fighters. His pilot, Dick Christie, was killed but Arthur and his two fellow crew members were finally picked up by a Royal Navy rescue launch. On this occasion there was a rare moment of chivalry, when a Junkers Ju88 spotted the craft but the pilot realised it was a rescue launch and waved before departing the scene.[3]

Arthur's first impressions of Sculthorpe were not flattering after the permanent and comfortable quarters at Swanton. He found a bleak and windswept collection of Nissen huts and the mess was so cold at early breakfasts that he had difficulty holding a knife and fork. However he soon appreciated the challenge of the Mosquito, with its *Gee* set device, a radio navigation system which greatly assisted navigation at low-level. In addition, the aircraft carried a powerful punch, with four 500lb bombs, two in the bomb bay and one under each wing. There were four .303 Browning machine guns mounted in the nose and four 20mm cannon, which when fired would vibrate the aircraft violently and fill the cockpit with smoke. The speed and manoeuvrability of the aircraft, even with one engine cut, was a revelation to the young navigator.[4]

THE FIRST OPERATIONS OF THE WING

By the start of October, the constant training in bombing practice and formation flying had paid off and the Wing was ready for its first operation. On Sunday 3 October, twenty-four aircraft from 464 and 487 Squadrons made low-level attacks on Mur-Le-Bretagne and Pont Château transformer stations in northern France. Pickard led 487 Squadron and Wing Commander Meakin 464 Squadron. Embry as usual was determined to see at first hand the results of all the planning and preparation

Group Capt. Pickard and his navigator Flt Lt John Broadley with Mosquito. Both were later killed in February 1944. (After the Battle)

and flew as 'tail-end Charlie' with his newly appointed SASO (Senior Air Staff Officer), Wing Commander David Atcherley, as navigator.[5] Embry flew in the guise of 'Wing Commander Smith', the assumed name being adopted as he had already escaped from captivity and if recaptured would have been a marked man, not least because he had killed a German soldier while escaping. For his part, Atcherley was flying with his arm in plaster as the result of a more than usually violent mess game.

All returned safely but Group Captain Pickard and his navigator, Flight Lieutenant John Broadley, in Mosquito 'F' for Freddie. They had engine problems on the return leg and were forced to make landfall at Predannack in Cornwall, with one engine out of action. Embry produced a large duck which had hit his Mosquito on the return leg – an occupational hazard in this type of low flying. He consulted the naturalist Peter Scott to plot the likely routes of migrating birds to minimise problems in the future.

Only days later the Wing suffered a severe mauling when twenty-four aircraft from 464 and 487 Squadrons were tasked to attack the Woippy aero engine works near Metz. Three aircraft from 487 Squadron and one from 464 failed to return. In addition, Mosquito HX 917 of Wing Commander A.G. Wilson, CO of 487 Squadron, was hit by flak near Thielt in Belgium and his navigator, Flying Officer D. Bridgeman, was killed.[6] Wilson made an emergency landing at Manston, severely shaken by the ordeal.

AIRFIELD DEVELOPMENT

On 15 September 1943, Sculthorpe achieved independent status and was no longer a satellite of West Raynham, but in these early months airfield infrastructure displayed all the signs of work in progress. Presumably there was some form of pecking order when it came to the allocation of billets. This appears to have been the fate of some personnel from the RAF regiment, detached from Nos. 2755 and 2836 Squadrons, arriving in early October and to be accommodated under canvas.

There seemed to be little protection from the vagaries of the north Norfolk weather, for a thunderstorm on 20 October turned the airfield into what amounted to a sea-plane base – 'water, water, everywhere, not a drop to drink' – with telephones out of order and some roofs of billets lifted off.[7] The adverse weather may have been a factor in causing three Mosquito accidents due to overshot landings on the airfield on 22 and 23 October. There were no fatalities, and the fact that the cockpits remained intact and no fire broke out was reassuring to the crews and increased their confidence in the aircraft's design and structure.

By 7 November there was the first touch of winter weather with a bitterly cold north-west wind, rain and sleet, and there was little improvement into December. On clear days there was fog to contend with which limited the scope of flying training and operations. On 17 November a new Officers' Mess opened, a sign of better things to come.

THE WING GETS INTO ITS STRIDE

Attacks on railways, power stations and airfields in northern France and north-west Germany were on the list for 140 Wing during the final months of 1943, even as winter was drawing in.

A Mosquito of 21 Squadron was lost on 27 November on an operation to north-west Germany. Flying Officer Thomas Shearer and his navigator, Flying Officer Robert Stirling, were both killed. Only two days later on the 29th a 464 Squadron aircraft on detachment at Ford in Sussex crashed in the sea after attacking airfields in northern France and the two crew were killed, Flying Officer Barry and Flight Sergeant Walsh. During the latter part of 1943 the Wing frequently operated from forward airfields like Ford, Predannack in Cornwall and Bradwell in Essex, which were nearer to their target areas than Sculthorpe.

On 30 November, three 487 Squadron aircraft were ordered to fly to Predannack to attack the blockade runner *Pietro Orseleo* which had been sighted along the coast of France. By the time the aircraft arrived at Predannack it was too late in the afternoon to mount an attack and the operation was postponed until the next day. By then two of the aircraft were unserviceable and Squadron Leader Alan Cussens made the decision to set off alone for the planned rendezvous with the fighter escort of Typhoons. Reaching the target, he ignored the very heavy fire and pressed home his attack to get his bombs to within 20ft of the ship, causing severe damage before being shot down and killed in the process. For this daring feat he received a Mention in Despatches, although there was a strong belief at the time that he should have been awarded a posthumous Victoria Cross.[8] Cussens' name is recorded on the Runnymede Memorial to the Missing and his navigator, Flying Officer Mackay, is buried in Guidel Communal Cemetery.

On 10 December, two Mosquitoes from 487 Squadron failed to return from intensive attacks over north-west Germany. Six aircraft set off to attack shipping on the Rhine, splitting up en route over Vlieland in the northern Netherlands, at which point two aircraft peeled off to attack a target in Holland. They were never seen again – Flying Officer Frankson and Flight Sergeant Thomas Mair in Mosquitoes 'D' and 'O'. Frankson and his navigator, Pilot Officer David Cake, were buried at Emmen (Nieuw Dordrecht) Cemetery. Flight Sergeant Mair and his navigator, Warrant Officer K. Blow, were laid to rest in Den Ham General Cemetery.[9]

During the month, the newly appointed CO of No. 617 ('Dam Busters') Squadron, Wing Commander Leonard Cheshire, came to Sculthorpe to visit Pickard, the acknowledged expert on low-level pinpoint bombing. Cheshire was developing the technique with his squadron and had his eye on the fast and manoeuvrable Mosquito to mark targets with greater accuracy than could be achieved with the Lancaster heavy bomber. After a short flight in the Mosquito VI Cheshire was convinced, but was assured by Pickard that Mosquitoes were harder to come by than diamonds. In due course, Cheshire was able to pull the necessary strings with higher authority, and obtained his Mosquito.

Intelligence had reached Air Chief Marshal Harris, AOC Bomber Command, that launch sites were being prepared in northern France for pilotless aircraft or rockets. Under the code name Operation 'Crossbow' the sites would become priority targets for Bomber Command and the Mosquito Wing. The task was so important that Embry came in person to brief the crews at Sculthorpe, equipped with a top-secret model of the sites in the Pas de Calais area. In his typical fashion he announced that the targets were to be destroyed 'at all costs' and, as Arthur Eyton-Jones recalled, 'when he (Embry) said the "at all costs" bit he looked at us with his piercing steel-blue eyes in a manner that I shall never forget …'[10]

The Sculthorpe Wing took off on 21 December for the first attack against the flying-bomb sites, in no doubt that these represented a serious threat to invasion plans. The visibility was so poor that the aircraft were recalled. On successive days, further operations were carried out, long before the public were aware of the threat. On the last day of the year, the Wing joined another formation in an attack on Le Ploy in France whilst en route to their new base at Hunsdon in Hertfordshire, a location closer to their designated targets. In early January 1944, Embry and his 2 Group headquarters vacated Bylaugh Hall, Dereham, and took over Mongewell Park in Berkshire. For No. 140 Wing, the time at Sculthorpe had been a mere dress rehearsal for what lay ahead of them. Lessons had been learned, often the hard way.

Sadly, Group Captain Pickard was killed only weeks later on 18 February 1944 while leading the attack on the Gestapo Prison at Amiens, code-named Operation 'Jericho'. Both he and his navigator, Flight Lieutenant John Broadley, are buried in St Pierre Cemetery in Amiens.[11]

Arthur Eyton-Jones continued to serve with 21 Squadron and was awarded the DFC in May 1944. Later he was responsible for training Mosquito navigators until demobilisation from the RAF in the rank of flight lieutenant in 1945. After the war he settled in the Wirral and took up a senior position in business until his retirement. He died on 16 March 2013 at the age of 92.[12]

NO. 100 GROUP (JANUARY TO MAY 1944)

By the end of 1943 and the start of 1944, the 2 Group squadrons had vacated north Norfolk for airfields further south. It was decided to move the recently formed No. 100 Group to these airfields, including Sculthorpe, and set up the headquarters in Bylaugh Hall. The group, established in November 1943, had the aim of organising electronic countermeasures against enemy defences in support of our bomber operations, literally 'Bomber Support', with the appropriate motto 'Confound and Destroy'.

Radar and other electronic devices had been in development since the start of the war with our early warning radar in the Battle of Britain. But now that Bomber Command was on the offensive, every means possible had to be found to jam and disrupt enemy ground radar and night fighter communications. The newly formed group was eventually to control eight airfields with 260 aircraft, which included Mosquitoes, acting as night fighter intruders, with Halifaxes, Stirlings, Fortresses and Liberators for radio countermeasures (RCM).

It was Sculthorpe's first taste of a secret world of electronic deception and subterfuge which was to have such importance later in the Cold War of the 1950s and 1960s, but it was to be a brief one, lasting a mere five months.

The first move was made in early January when No. 214 Squadron, based at Downham Market with Stirlings, was transferred from 3 Group to 100 Group and ordered to move to Sculthorpe for designation as a Special Duties (SD) unit and for conversion to the Flying Fortress B-17F, which was deemed more suitable for the new role. The first squadron personnel arrived on 16 January and, in a foretaste of things to come, a unit called the 'American Detachment' under the command of Captain G.E. Paris moved into Sculthorpe to organise training on the new aircraft.

No. 214 Squadron (Federated Malay States) badge. Motto 'Ultor in umbris' – 'Avenging in the shadows'. The nightjar in the badge is a bird which is active at night and illustrates the role of the squadron.

In early February the first personnel arrived from the USAAF 96th Bombardment Group, based at Snetterton Heath, to carry out modifications which included flame dampers for engine exhausts suitable for night flying, and to fit electronic equipment such as *Gee* navigational sets, and *Mandrel* and *Carpet*, devices for jamming German radar emissions.

By the end of March, the American Detachment had completed much of the initial training work and the unit was redesignated the 803rd Bombardment Squadron (Provisional), at first under the command of Captain Paris, with a strength of six Fortresses. Paris handed over to a new commander in April, Major (later Lieutenant Colonel) C.A. Scott. In the meantime, a fresh RAF unit took over the task of converting crews, No. 1699 (Fortress Training) Flight.

By April, No. 214 Squadron was operating a total of twenty-one B-17 Flying Fortresses, of which fourteen were the B-17F models, and the remaining seven the G-models. There was a single Fortress I AN520 which had been with 90 Squadron in 1941 and was to remain at Sculthorpe until it was scrapped in September 1944.[13] On 20 April, No. 214 Squadron was declared fully operational.

By this time, personnel at Sculthorpe included 104 RAF officers, 233 senior RAF NCOs and 705 airmen. The Women's Auxiliary Air Force (WAAF) section comprised 5 officers, 9 senior NCOs and 176 airwomen. The US contingent totalled 39 officers, 100 senior NCOs and 934 airmen.

The units began operating from about 26 April but there were few incidents until 7 May when a 214 Squadron aircraft claimed its first success against an attacking Me109 night fighter, which was claimed to be damaged in the encounter.

Sculthorpe's war was nearly over, as the station had been chosen for upgrading to Very Heavy Bomber Base (VHB) status. The three flying units and the RAF regiment contingent prepared to move to Oulton along with their technical and other stores. By 16 May, the process was complete and the contractors moved in. Empty Nissen huts at No. 3 Site were allocated for the accommodation of workmen. The station was placed on a care and maintenance basis, thus ending a short but eventful period in the airfield's life.

NOTES

1.   Henry, Mike, DFC, *Air Gunner,* p.158.
2.   Bruce Anderson (ed.), *Ploughshares and Propellers* (RAF Museum), extract from Fg Off. Harvey Cocks.
3.   *Daily Telegraph,* Arthur Eyton-Jones obit. 3 June 2013.
4.   Eyton-Jones, Arthur, *Day Bomber* (Sutton Publishing Ltd, 1998), p.108.
5.   David was the twin brother of Wg Cdr D.F.W. 'Batchy' Atcherley of Fighter Command.
6.   Bridgeman was later buried at Brookwood Cemetery.
7.   AIR 28/692 Operations Record Book: Sculthorpe.

8. Bowyer, M.J.F., *2 Group RAF,* pp.346–7.

9. Eyton-Jones pp.118–19.

10. Eyton-Jones p.121–2.

11. For a fuller account of the careers of Gp Capt. Pickard and ACM Embry see author's book *Flying Lives with a Norfolk Theme.*

12. *Daily Telegraph,* obit. 3 June 2013.

13. Streetly, Martin, *Confound and Destroy,* p.41.

3. AIRFIELD DEVELOPMENT (1944–49)

CONVERSION TO VERY HEAVY BOMBER (VHB) AIRFIELD

On 16 May 1944, the last flying units vacated the airfield, as it was now listed for reconstruction as a Very Heavy Bomber Station.

All the original runways were torn up and new 300ft wide and substantially stronger runways were laid down. The main 00-18 was 3,000 yards long and the others both 2,000 yards. Major reconstruction work was not completed before the end of the war and thereafter some facilities still had to be finished.

In the meantime, there were major changes in two of the public road alignments and a farm during this period. The A1067 (Norwich to Hunstanton road) which linked Fakenham with Dunton Patch and Syderstone was closed as it now crossed the airfield. Brazen Hall Farm was demolished to make way for the new runways. The A148 road from Fakenham to Rudham and then on to King's Lynn had to be realigned from Dunton Patch in the direction of Tattersett, and this new road was termed 'the Burma Road'. This was completed in 1944 and is visible on the aerial photograph of 1946 but not on the Ordnance Survey map until the version of 1954 (OS Sheet 125 Fakenham). This so-called 'Burma Road' took its name from the road first constructed in the Far East in the late 1930s between Burma and south-west China as the lifeline for the beleaguered Chinese during the Sino-Japanese war. The 'Burma Road' name may also have been a poignant reminder of the tragic fate of so many men from the Norfolk Regiment, part of the 18th Division, who were captured by the Japanese after the fall of Singapore in 1942. Later in the 1950s there was a further realignment of the road to the south-west of the airfield (the present B1454) to replace the closed portion of the A1067 (see also plans on pp.178–9).

The actual airfield redevelopment appeared to stop during 1945 or 1946, resuming around 1948 at the height of the Cold War.

These years were recalled by Roland Axman, who lived locally at the time. Taylor Woodrow was the main contractor during the period and he remembered the lorries driving through the village of Docking, backwards and forwards from Snettisham beach, carrying sand and shingle to extend the runways prior to the Americans coming.

Extending the runway in 1945. Two employees of John Laing & Sons, building contractors. On right is Geoffrey Minns from Pulham St Mary, who had also worked at Manston airfield in Kent. (Gary Windeler)

There were hundreds of Irish labourers on-site living in a campsite of temporary wooden huts, about forty or so to a hut, working day and night, or so it seemed. Roland worked for Waggs the Bakers in Docking and he used to take vanloads of bread to Sculthorpe for the workers – barrowloads of bread were shuttled between the bread store and the van. Two workers were responsible for using what looked like a bacon slicer to slice up the large quartern loaves, a task that took them all day, and then the bread was taken by the bucketful to the workers on the site. They probably had their own bars on site so there was no trouble locally as the Irishmen seemed to stay on the base.

During 1948, the airfield had not formally been reopened but was used by Ansons of No. 1510 BABS (Beam Approach Beacon System) Flight based at Bircham Newton. Sculthorpe possessed paved runways, landing lights and many of the modern airfield facilities which Bircham Newton lacked and was also a useful storage facility. Cliff Howard, an AC1 instrument fitter based at Bircham Newton in 1948, recalled being sent to Sculthorpe to assist with a night flying exercise. On this occasion, an Anson was started up inside a hangar, with a resulting massive burst of smoke, noise and dust everywhere.

4. A SECOND FRIENDLY INVASION

'The supreme art of war is to subdue the enemy without fighting.'

(Sun Tzu, *The Art of War*)

Sculthorpe's life as an active station during the Second World War had been brief, but its development as a Very Heavy Bomber airfield during the later 1940s signalled a fresh role. What was this new role and how did Sculthorpe fit into the bigger picture of an increasingly dangerous and uncertain world?

THE COLD WAR AND THE FIRST AMERICAN DEPLOYMENTS

Distrust of the Soviet Union under Stalin existed long before the war ended in May 1945. The collapse of Germany and the advance of Soviet forces into the heart of Europe had created a new political situation. It left the Soviet Union in a dominating position in Eastern Europe, including the Baltic states: Poland, Czechoslovakia, Romania and the eastern half of Germany including Berlin. This seemed to be underwritten by the Western Allies at the Potsdam Conference of August 1945, including the agreement to divide Germany into 'zones', one for each of the victorious powers. Berlin, situated in the heart of the Soviet Zone of East Germany, would be divided into sectors, with the agreement that there would be access for the Western Allies into Berlin via a narrow land corridor through the Soviet Zone.

Stalin had obviously no intention of relaxing his grip on his conquests in Eastern Europe, but the question now arose: would it end there? In 1946, the Soviet Union still had six million men and women under arms and maintained its military arsenal at the wartime level, whereas the Western Allies had already started to demobilise front-line forces. Much of Eastern Europe had become an armed camp under the domination of the Soviet Union, and any hope for free elections was crushed, for example in Poland. Winston Churchill summed up the international situation in a speech at Fulton, Missouri, in March 1946, when he warned that 'from Stettin to Trieste an "Iron Curtain" has descended across Europe'. The term 'Cold War' began to be used to describe the state of relations between the Soviet Union and the Western Allies.

In theory there was little to stop Soviet forces from advancing right through to the English Channel, except that the West had one trump card, the possession of the atomic bomb, which the United States had developed during the Manhattan Project. This was a research programme begun in 1942 jointly by the United States, Britain and Canada to develop the atomic bomb. The first atomic test had taken place in the desert of New Mexico on 17 July 1945 and only three weeks later, on 6 August, an atomic bomb was dropped on the Japanese city of Hiroshima, killing 78,000 people and seriously injuring another 90,000. A second bomb was dropped on the city of Nagasaki three days later, killing nearly 80,000 people. On 14 August, the Japanese surrendered to the Allies.

These early atomic bombs, code-named 'Fat Man', were few in number and cumbersome, weighing 10,000lbs, and there was only one unit fully trained and equipped to deliver them, the B-29 Superfortresses of the 509th Composite Group.[1] The hope was that the Soviets would be kept guessing as to true US capabilities, typical of the game of bluff and counterbluff that was to feature so often during the Cold War.

There was no way that the Western Allies could match man-for-man the Soviet armed forces. There was pressure to reduce troop commitments in Europe both at home and in the United States, not least because of the financial drain on resources. Air power was the only viable option and the best hope seemed to lie with the B-29 Superfortresses of the recently created US Strategic Air Command (SAC), which would be required to reinforce the relatively small force of RAF Avro Lincoln bombers in the event of war in Europe. The problem was that that the B-29, although in many ways superior to the Lincoln (which was an advanced version of the wartime Lancaster), still lacked the essential intercontinental range, so a foothold or two in Europe for the US Army Air Force was going to be essential.

In March 1946, the last of the US Eighth Air Force B-17 Flying Fortresses left Honington in Suffolk. Building on the trust that had developed between Britain and the United States since Operation 'Overlord', the cross-channel invasion of Europe, there was an informal agreement between General Carl Spaatz, Commanding General of the US Army Air Force, and Air Chief Marshal Lord Tedder, Chief of the Air Staff, that in the event of an international emergency permission would be granted by the UK government for US bombers to use certain British bases. Later that month, four B-29 Superfortresses arrived at Marham to conduct joint bombing exercises with the RAF in Project 'Ruby'. These involved testing a variety of very heavy bombs developed for the RAF during the war against the former Nazi U-boat pens in Kiel, Germany.

The question arose as to which airfields would be the most suitable for the deployments, especially with the minimum runway requirements for the B-29 of at least

8,000ft in length, 200ft in width and 1,000ft available for overruns, plus other allied facilities, hardstandings and hangars. There were several possibilities: Manston in Kent, Filton near Bristol and Boscombe Down in Wiltshire. In East Anglia there were a number of airfields which had been chosen for upgrading to Very Heavy Bomber (VHB) status in 1944, including Scampton, Waddington, Marham, Mildenhall, Lakenheath and Sculthorpe. North Creake had also been earmarked but this had been cancelled. The East Anglian airfields were deemed most appropriate for the task ahead but the huge requirements of hardstandings and accommodation for a complete B-29 bomber group of three squadrons would be beyond the capacity even of the VHB airfields on the list, as RAF requirements fell somewhat short of the American need to 'think big'. It was accepted that the squadrons of a complete bomber group would likely have to be split between two bases at any one time, creating some complications for command and control. Of the airfields judged to be most suitable, Lakenheath and Sculthorpe had special buildings and other facilities constructed, in the bomb dumps and in the technical areas, to enable the 10,000lb atomic bomb to be assembled on-site and then loaded into the specially adapted B-29s, should atomic weapons ever be required for deployment in Britain.[2]

In August 1946, the McMahon Act (Atomic Energy Act) was passed by the US Congress, which prohibited the passing of information or help on atomic matters to any other nation including Britain. In spite of this, the same month saw the arrival in Britain of US engineering specialists to oversee the necessary atomic constructions, which were virtually completed by early 1947.[3]

During 1947, US bomber detachments became more frequent, with one to Germany in May followed by the first deployment to England in June, when nine B-29s from the 340th Bomb Squadron, 97th Bomb Group, flew into Marham as part of a week-long tour to commemorate the arrival of the 97th BG to England in 1942.

DEEPENING CRISIS

By early 1948, the international situation showed no signs of improvement and there were many reasons for increased tension between east and west. The Soviet Union was busy establishing client states in the conquered territories of Eastern Europe, for example in Czechoslovakia, where a Soviet-backed coup brought a communist regime to power. Pressure was building for a more systematic arrangement for the placement of US bombers in Britain, even on a temporary basis – for example, a complete group of three squadrons rather than merely a handful of aircraft from time to time.

The sense of crisis deepened with the Berlin crisis of June 1948 when the Soviets closed down all land routes from the western zones of Germany into Berlin as a prelude, or so it was believed at the time, to a complete Soviet takeover of the city. The Western Allies had either to abandon the city or to mount a massive airlift via the three 20-mile-wide air corridors from their zones into Berlin. The latter option was chosen and Operation 'Vittles' started on 26 June, lasting until May of the following year when the Russians finally backed down.

The Berlin crisis was the catalyst for the US and UK governments to agree on more effective arrangements for USAF deployments in Britain whereby two bomb groups, each of thirty B-29s, would fly to England for temporary duty (TDY) for the duration of the crisis. For various logistical reasons Scampton was the first to receive thirty B-29s of the 28th Bomb Group on 17 July, followed by the 307th Bomb Group to Marham and the 2nd Bomb Group to Lakenheath by August – a total of around ninety bombers. At present, this was a non-nuclear capability designed to act as a deterrent should the Russians be tempted to advance into the western sectors of Germany. Supply and maintenance facilities would be provided at Burtonwood in Cheshire by the 59th Air Depot Wing. The USAAF had used the base during the war years but the main task was now to supervise the massive airlift operations into Berlin.

It was anticipated that TDY for the Strategic Air Command bomb groups would be for 90-day periods on a rotational basis and for the purposes of operational control a new command structure was established in August 1948, the Third Air Division (Provisional), with headquarters at Marham. In September, the 'Provisional' label was dropped and the headquarters moved to Bushy Park near London, signalling a more permanent structure. The divisional commander was Major General Leon W. Johnson, a highly decorated officer and no stranger to Norfolk, as he had commanded the 44th Bomb Group at Shipdham during the war.

By the end of 1948 the foundations had been laid for what was to become a per-manent USAF presence on British soil for the first time in peacetime. On the local front, Sculthorpe had reopened in December 1948 with lengthened runways and new extended facilities. Officially a satellite of Marham, the base was being administered on a care and maintenance basis. On 16 December 1948, preparations were in hand to open Sculthorpe for the arrival of the first US Air Force units expected in February 1949. Wing Commander L.B.B. King commanded the advance party during a period of intense activity to make the station ready for the new era.

NOTES

1.   Around nine bombs were available in July 1946 and approximately fifty bombs in 1948. About thirty B-29 Superfortresses were converted to drop atomic weapons (*The Unsinkable Aircraft Carrier*, Duncan Campbell, p.28).
2.   Young, Prof. Ken, 'US atomic capability and the British forward bases in the Cold War', *Journal of Contemporary History* 42(1), Jan. 2007 pp.117–36.
3.   Private information.

5. BOMBERS ARRIVE (1949)

'Don't criticize the food, beer and cigarettes. They don't like them any more than we do ...'

(From US Third Air Division 'Do's and Don'ts' for American airmen, 1948)

92ND BOMB GROUP (MEDIUM) USAF

It must have been quite a moment for those present at Sculthorpe on the afternoon of Monday 7 February 1949, for the first B-29 Superfortresses of the 92nd Bomb Group (Medium) were due to land at any moment in what was to be the first American deployment there since the airfield reopened.

There had been intensive work at the base for well over a year building up stores and equipment. In early January, Sculthorpe became a self-accounting unit for No. 3 Group RAF Bomber Command with the task of administering a Heavy Bomber Group of the United States Air Force. New airmen's blocks were being constructed (the 'Z' blocks) with single men's cubicle accommodation,[1] and there had been progress in the construction of the airmen's married quarters. The station had been unoccupied for over four years and much of it was damp and in a poor state of repair. There was still 'work in progress', with brick-hutted accommodation and Nissen huts which compared unfavourably even with pre-war bomber stations. The NAAFI (Navy, Army and Air Force Institutes) had just opened, but with Fakenham the nearest town of any size, first impressions must have looked bleak to many young servicemen and women. Even the cinema had been closed due to a faulty roof.

By the end of January 1949 the station workshops had opened and there had been deliveries of 700 bombs, each of 500lbs, to the bomb stores. RAF personnel numbered 17 officers and 351 other ranks. In early February an advance party of personnel from the 92nd Bomb Group arrived to complete the final preparations.

At about 4.30 p.m. on 7 February, the first two aircraft touched down, having flown from their base at Spokane in Washington County, USA, via Bermuda. Bad weather had forced six of the aircraft to divert to Lyneham in Wiltshire and the first pilot to land reported that he had difficulty in locating the runways at Sculthorpe due to poor visibility.[2]

Since 1948, the Americans had been lobbying hard for a firmer foothold in the UK than could be offered by the system of rotational deployments, but the British government had to consider the thorny question of the costs and also the strength of public opinion. January and February 1949 saw the most tense period of the Berlin Airlift, with the tonnage of supplies being flown to the city at record levels in spite of continual harassment by the Soviet authorities. The threat of war over the issue could not be ruled out. Negotiations were proceeding for other bases, for example in the Midlands, but for the moment it had been decided to use Marham, Lakenheath and the newly opened Sculthorpe for US bomber deployments, with Scampton or Waddington in Lincolnshire earmarked for fighter units.

The Berlin crisis had certainly removed many of the doubts about the American presence but the issue had to be treated carefully in case the impression was given that the UK had become the USA's 49th state! It was made clear that the Americans would only send B-29s to Britain at the clear invitation of the British government with non-nuclear weaponry at their disposal. At first the deployments were to be for 'temporary duty' as part of long-range flight training, but in an *Eastern Daily Press* report of 19 January 1949, 'well-informed quarters in Washington' were quoted as saying that 'as long as the "cold war" with Russia continued the Superfortresses were here to stay'.[3]

Within a few days the 92nd Bomb Group was established at Sculthorpe. The unit had been based at Polebrook in Northamptonshire during 1942 before moving to the Mediterranean and serving with great distinction during the invasions of Sicily and Italy, earning two Distinguished Unit Citations (DCUs) in the process. It was now the responsibility of the station commander at Sculthorpe, Group Captain H.C. Parker, to ensure that the Americans were able to settle in and begin to operate effectively. Overnight, the station strength had increased to over 500 RAF personnel, 181 USAF officers and 712 enlisted men. Units present comprised the 7502nd Base Complement Squadron for the administrative role and three squadrons of the Bomb Group, each of ten aircraft, the 325th, 326th and 327th Bomb Squadrons.

An information and brochure guide was issued to the new arrivals with a summary of the local facilities and a welcoming message from Group Captain Parker which included the assurance that 'we will try and make you as comfortable as circumstances permit'. Various hotels, licensed and unlicensed, in Hunstanton, Fakenham and Norwich were listed, with tariffs for long and short stays. The Le Strange Arms and Golf Links Hotel in Old Hunstanton offered accommodation at twenty-five shillings (25s) per day in winter and thirty shillings (30s) in the summer.[4] The Dell Hotel in Castle Hill in Norwich charged twelve shillings and six pence (12*s* 6*d*) for bed and breakfast, with an inclusive fee of just over six pounds per week (or eighteen shillings per day). The Royal Hotel in Norwich had single beds available daily at ten shillings and six pence, with doubles from one pound. Evening buses to Norwich were to be arranged when required from Sculthorpe, for which airmen would pay the return fare of six pence.

What could not be denied was the discrepancy between the average pay of the USAF personnel and that of the RAF national servicemen, many of whom were in post at Sculthorpe from 1948. This also applied to civilians, who had been enduring a food-rationing regime since the war. In the period 1950–51 the average weekly wage in the UK was around eight pounds, eight shillings (£8 8*s*), or approximately £34 monthly. At the start of the 1950s, agricultural wages (of vital importance in the economy of Norfolk) ranged from a minimum of just over 22 shillings (£1 2*s*) weekly to four pounds, fourteen shillings (£4 14*s*) weekly. At the same time, the *minimum* monthly rate for a USAF enlisted man with limited service was $80, or £28 to £30 (calculated by the then fixed dollar/sterling exchange rate of $2.80 to the £).[5] RAF regular ground crew would earn a minimum of between £10 and £11 monthly and the national service airmen at least one pound less. The minimum pay a USAF officer could expect was $213 monthly (or around £76 to £77), whereas an acting plot officer (aircrew) could earn between £16 and £17. So as a rule of thumb, the American airman was anything up to three times better off than his British counterpart.

Some of these issues were covered in a list of 'Do's and Don'ts' drawn up by the Third Air Division in the autumn of 1948:

> … You are higher paid than British airmen. Don't rub it in. Never forget that you are the highest-paid military service in the world … Don't criticize the food, beer and cigarettes. They don't like them any more than we do. They have had to put up with rationing for almost nine years.[6]

At Sculthorpe, immediate arrangements had to be made for catering, customs, currency exchange and directional signs. The previous RAF Officers' Mess had now become The Officers' Club, with the RAF and USAF officers messing together. There was much pressure on accommodation for the married American airmen and their families who had to occupy the RAF married quarters. Sporting facilities were limited and use had to be made of Syderstone's village football pitch for the time being.

The basic living conditions and lack of amenities were blamed for some of the petty crime that surfaced from time to time. Sculthorpe had responsibility for RAF Little Snoring, whose buildings had also fallen into disrepair since the end of the war and was the subject of frequent pilfering due to the absence of any servicemen at the site. Matters were made more complicated by a gentleman called Mr Massingham, who was squatting in a bungalow on the perimeter track of the airfield at Little Snoring.

All attempts to recover rents or presumably to move him on had proved fruitless. The airfield site had been earmarked for storage, possibly even of explosive materials, but it seems that he refused to budge in the face of the combined powers of the Royal Air Force and the United States Air Force.

On 11 February 1949, Major General Leon W. Johnson, the Third Air Division commander, paid a visit to Sculthorpe to welcome the personnel, touring the airfield and facilities with the commander of the 92nd, Colonel S.E. Manzo, accompanied by Air Vice-Marshal Hesketh, AOC of No. 3 RAF Bomber Group. There was an informal reception at the Crown Hotel in Fakenham hosted by the Fakenham Chamber of Commerce on 17 February, for members of the 92nd. The President, Mr J.A. Keith, paid tribute to the part played by the Americans during the war and added: 'Only by America and Britain standing shoulder to shoulder will Christianity, freedom and peace remain in the world.'[7]

Welcome proceedings were marred by an early mishap on the base, a fatal accident on 23 February in which an airman, Corporal Turcell, was killed while cleaning guns on a B-29. The gun had been fired by accident.

Formalities were the order of the day in a colour hoisting ceremony on 12 March when the Stars and Stripes and Union Jack were raised jointly on the flagpole for the first time.

There was a heightened state of readiness due to increased international tension over the Berlin Airlift, so there was a full programme of flying training and bombing practise during March and April. Typical targets included Heligoland, captured from the Germans at the war's end and now used by the RAF and USAF as a bombing range. Kidlington in Oxfordshire and Wainfleet in Lincolnshire were also targeted for practice bombing runs. By the middle of May, the 92nd had completed this deployment at Sculthorpe and returned to its home base of Spokane in Washington State.

98TH BOMB WING (MEDIUM)

By this time the aircraft and personnel of the 98th Bomb Wing had begun to arrive at Sculthorpe on a 90-day deployment (TDY – temporary duty), from their base at Spokane via Iceland, Bermuda and Lagens in the Azores. The Wing, commanded by Colonel Richard D. Dick, comprised B-29s of Nos. 343, 344 and 345 Squadrons and had been reactivated as a unit on 1 July 1947. The Wing had already served a TDY posting in Okinawa, during which two B-29s had crashed and a number of personnel had been lost when a C-54 ditched in the Pacific. Training assignments at Sculthorpe included liaison with No. 12 Group of the Royal Air Force. The other East Anglian bases of Marham and Lakenheath saw the arrival of the 509th Bomb Wing, whose B-29s attracted particular interest as the unit had been responsible for dropping the atomic bombs on Japan and were fully trained and equipped for the delivery of nuclear weapons – 'Silverplate' being the code word for 'atomic capable' aircraft.

Boeing B-29 of the 98th Bomb Group on the perimeter track. The unit was based at Sculthorpe from May to August 1949. 'Y' symbol denotes group number. Just visible in the background are the control tower and hangars. In the foreground is probably a sugar beet crop. (Gary Windeler)

Although May saw the ending of the Berlin Blockade, all RAF and USAF units were being held at the highest state of readiness. The previous March the Western European nations of the UK, France, Belgium, Luxembourg and the Netherlands had joined together in a self-defence pact by signing the Treaty of Brussels. On 4 April, the North Atlantic Treaty was signed, establishing NATO and bringing together eleven nations, including those from Western Europe, with Canada and the USA in a mutual defence treaty. On 15 April 1949, the headquarters of the Third Air Division moved from Bushy Park to South Ruislip, partly to be closer to Northolt airfield (the 59th Air Depot Wing support organisation was based at Burtonwood).

It was against this background that Strategic Air Command's 90-day TDYs were conducted in East Anglia, and there was no let-up in the intensity of operations. At Sculthorpe, the role of the RAF personnel was merely to assist in the administration of the base while the USAF had complete control over operational requirements. Developments at the airfield included the installation of GCA (Ground Control Approach) and Contact Lighting – high- and low-intensity approach lights (completed on all runways by January 1950). There were still equipment shortages but airmen's accommodation continued to improve. By the end of July 1949 the number of airmen-type married quarters had reached sixty-two, and three of six planned airmen-type single cubicle barrack blocks (the 'Z' blocks) had been completed, each to accommodate 100 personnel.

A major air exercise code-named 'Foil' involving the combined forces of the RAF and the US Air Force units, including the 98th Bomb Wing, took place from Saturday 25 June until Sunday 3 July. The aim was to test the effectiveness of fighter defence against the bombers. The operation was directed by Air Marshal Sir Basil Embry, now AOC-in-C RAF Fighter Command based at No. 11 Group headquarters, Uxbridge. With over 500 aircraft taking part, the exercise was one of the largest to have taken place in the post-war period. In addition to British and American participation, Meteors from the Royal Netherlands Air Force formed part of the fighter formations.

The exercise was divided into three phases, each involving mock attacks by RAF Lincolns, Lancasters and Wellingtons, with Mosquitoes as target markers together with USAF B-29 bombers, ranging over large areas of southern England and Wales. Then it was up to the fighters to carry out rapid and accurate interceptions.

Correspondents of *Flight* magazine were on board some of the 'twenty-nines', as they called the B-29 bombers, on the first phase of the exercise from Sculthorpe on Saturday 25 June. The first leg was flown by three of the 'Superforts', one each from 344, 345 and 343 Squadrons and commanded respectively by Major Birdsong, Major Arnold and Lieutenant Colonel Gray. Flying at 25,000ft and an average speed of 290mph towards Heligoland, the task was to drop a packet of six 500lb practice bombs on the target. Then followed the ascent to 35,000ft and return to British airspace over Harwich, heading for the turning point at Northampton towards the designated mock target of Birmingham for a camera bombing approach. A correspondent commented:

> Lulled by the warmth of the pressurized cabin (this equivalent altitude within was 14,600ft) and the smoothness of passage … we felt extremely complacent about high-altitude bombing. This was war in comfort.

There was some excitement when a Spitfire intercepted the aircraft over Northampton, the results of which would later be analysed in the camera-gun film but appeared to work to the advantage of the gunners. The Birmingham bomb run was followed by a similar exercise over Liverpool with attempted interceptions by two Meteors proving inconclusive.

The expected routine return to Sculthorpe proved otherwise for Colonel Gray's aircraft of 343 Squadron, due to a malfunction of the port inner engine causing severe vibration and a danger of it breaking away. In the resulting emergency and loss of height three of the crew and two correspondents, Charles Gardner of the BBC and Waldo Drake of the *Los Angeles Times* made premature parachute exits from the aircraft at 20,000ft, landing north of the Humber, fortunately without serious injuries. The aircraft was to land safely and the episode was later narrated by Charles Gardner on BBC *Radio Newsreel*.

On the Sunday, Sculthorpe's contribution to the exercise was twelve aircraft, targeting Heligoland before turning for the English coast to make mock attacks on London and Burtonwood, experiencing a number of interceptions by Meteors and Vampires. Once again, Colonel Gray's aircraft had problems with the port inner engine, which refused to feather, forcing the B-29 to land at Amsterdam. The correspondent concluded that in spite of some of the minor snags during the exercise, the B-29 groups 'constitute a powerful weapon, held in the hands of skilled and enthusiastic personnel'.[8]

The exercise had tested the logistics of the base, with scrambler phones installed, an extra 145,000 gallons of fuel delivered and fuel turnover totalling over a million gallons. Simulated combat conditions were observed on the ground including the diet for personnel, which consisted of dehydrated potatoes, powdered eggs, bully beef, month-old bread and the inevitable spam. However, the 98th were highly rated as a result of the exercise and declared fully combat ready.

The RAF complement on the station during July had declined slightly to 15 officers, 8 warrant officers, 23 senior NCOs and 382 airmen, while USAF personnel had increased to 186 officers and 823 enlisted men.[9]

The 98th completed their TDY at Sculthorpe by mid-August to return to Spokane, making way for the 63rd Bomb Squadron of the 43rd Bomb Group.

A NEW SQUADRON AND A NEW ERA

The news announced on 23 September 1949 that the Soviet Union had successfully tested an atomic bomb on 14 July came as a shock to Western governments. It had been known for some time that the Soviets were working on the bomb, possibly for production by the early 1950s, but this development changed the entire dynamic of international affairs. Intelligence leaks from the West and the capture of German scientists had produced the expertise required, but the Soviets were still some way from being able to deliver such a weapon in the event of war. If anything, the United States homeland was secure for the moment, but the United Kingdom was in the front line. Such a fact could not escape the planners of the British defence establishment.

Only weeks later the communists under Mao came to power in China, fuelling the notion that there was a massive communist conspiracy about to threaten Western interests east and west. This was bound to be reflected in defence planning, as events were to prove.

The 43rd Bomb Group, which arrived in East Anglia in mid-August brought with it the first appearance in this country of the Boeing B-50A Stratobomber, which was basically a larger version of the B-29 Superfortress with much extended capability. The aircraft was still on the restricted list and required floodlighting at night, which meant that Chance lights had to be used at the dispersals [Chance lights were powerful floodlights positioned at a number of locations around the airfield pointing in towards the centre to illuminate the landing area]. The three squadrons of the group were split, the 64th Bomb Squadron assigned to Marham, the 65th to Lakenheath and the 63rd to Sculthorpe, with the addition of three modified B-29s, termed KB-29M tankers, for in-flight refuelling purposes and based at Sculthorpe. These aircraft had their gun turrets removed and carried extra fuel in their bomb bays. The squadron at

Lucky Lady II at Sculthorpe 18 April 1949. (*Flightglobal Archive* 1 Sept. 1949, p.262)

Sculthorpe was commanded by Lieutenant Colonel R.W. Stanley and was noteworthy as the unit which included *Lucky Lady II*, the aircraft which had made the first non-stop 23,452-mile flight around the world between 26 February and 2 March. The record was made possible by in-flight refuelling at four points during the flight: the Azores, Dhahran (Saudi Arabia), the Philippines and Hawaii. Most of the fourteen crew who completed the 94-hour flight were still with the group, although only two remained with that aircraft. The message conveyed by the well-publicised news of the flight was clear – there is no corner of the globe that is beyond the reach of USAF Strategic Air Command.

A visit by Her Majesty Queen Mary on 9 September, accompanied by Lord and Lady Fermoy, provided an enjoyable diversion from the intensive routine of the 90-day TDY. There was continued improvement in social and recreational facilities. The cinema provided much of the in-house entertainment but there was also a music circle established. The station gardens were able to supply the Airmen's Mess with a welcome quantity of vegetables. Much had been achieved but there was still much to be done.

It was another busy operational period for the unit, culminating in Exercise 'Bulldog' over the weekend of 23 to 26 September. Commanded once again by Air Marshal Sir Basil Embry, AOC-in-C Fighter Command, this time the aim was to conduct an offensive bomber exercise, as distinct from the defensive fighter exercise of 'Foil'. Apart from RAF and USAF units, there was also participation from the Dutch, French and Belgian air forces. The scope of the exercise stretched from Scotland to the south-east of England.

In-flight refuelling was an important feature of the exercise, as demonstrated when on the Saturday afternoon the tankers were tasked to rendezvous at 25,000ft over Bremen, then to cross the east coast at Yarmouth in an attempt to act as a diversion for a bomber force, the main USAF formation, heading for the target objective of the Millwall dock area. On this occasion, the bombers were not sighted and no fighter interceptions took place.

By 18 November, the TDY of the 63rd was over and the aircraft returned to their home base of Tucson, Arizona, by way of the Azores.

NOTES

1. Field Marshal Montgomery, Chief of the Imperial General Staff (1946–48), allegedly insisted that all single servicemen and women should have single accommodation.
2. *Eastern Daily Press* (EDP), 8 Feb. 1949.
3. *EDP,* 19 Jan. 1949.
4. Present tariff for Le Strange Arms (Feb. 2012) is upwards of £60 for the day rate (single room) and £90 for a double. (Source: Le Strange website).
5. The fixed exchange rate of $2.80 to the £ was in place from 1950 until 1967.
6. Quote from Bowyer, M.J.F., *Force for Freedom*, p.29.
7. *EDP,* 18 Feb. 1949.
8. Flightglobal Archive, 30 June 1949, pp.752–4.
9. AIR 28/1110 Operations Record Book: RAF Sculthorpe, 1949–51.

6. HANDOVER TO THE AMERICANS (1949–51)

'Air power may either end war or end civilisation.'

(Winston Churchill, House of Commons, 14 March 1933)

The departure of the 63rd Bomb Squadron in November 1949 made way for the Boeing B-29s of the 19th Bomb Squadron of the 22nd Bomb Group for a three-month TDY from March Air Force Base, California. Of the remaining squadrons of the group, the 2nd went to Marham and the 33rd to Lakenheath. A further unit arrived at Sculthorpe on 22 December, the 23rd Strategic Reconnaissance Squadron of the 5th Strategic Reconnaissance Group from Fairfield-Suisun in California. Ten Boeing RB-29s, reconnaissance versions of the B-29 bomber, made up the complement by January 1950; a change from the more advanced Boeing B-50s and possibly even a retrograde step in terms of the aircraft capabilities.

Co-ordination between the Royal Air Force and USAF personnel did not always run as smoothly as had been hoped. At the end of December, Group Captain Parker complained that the Americans had the habit of keeping the movements of visiting squadrons to themselves, which hampered the arrangements for the reception of units. Also, nobody would reveal whether the bulk fuel installation was graded 100 or 145 octane fuel (the former being the requirement for the RB-29).[1] A party organised for the children of RAF and USAF personnel in the Sergeants' Mess must have come as light relief for all concerned, followed by some of the usual Christmas festivities.

In the meantime, negotiations were proceeding at the highest levels of government between the United States and Britain, with a view to sanctioning permanent US bases in this country and in other parts of Western Europe. There was already, of course, a permanent American presence in West Germany, but the addition of some bases in the UK was felt to be vital in any future emergency. The US Air Force Strategic Air Command favoured the stationing of three bomb wings to be distributed between Marham, Lakenheath and Sculthorpe, a total of ninety bombers. The target date for this was set for the summer of 1950 and preparations got under way by the start of the year. Many matters had to be resolved concerning the stationing of foreign forces in peacetime including the cost of upgrading facilities, issues concerning jurisdiction and customs, and the strength of public opinion when there was no immediate emergency.

There was also the need to reinforce RAF Bomber Command on the 'self-help' principle as it would be a number of years before the new generation of jet V-bombers would be available to replace the ageing Avro Lincoln (a development of the wartime Lancaster). The English Electric Canberra, a light jet bomber which lacked the range to penetrate Soviet territory, would not be in service before 1951. Accordingly, under the Mutual Defence Assistance Agreement signed with the Americans in January 1950, seventy B-29 bombers would be loaned to the RAF during the spring of 1950. The plan was for the B-29s (renamed 'Washingtons' in RAF service) to be delivered to each of Marham, Lakenheath and Sculthorpe for crew training before being formally organised into RAF squadrons.

At Sculthorpe, the 23rd Strategic Reconnaissance Squadron was training hard during the spring of 1950, with blind bombing practice on the ranges at Heston in Middlesex and Kidlington in Oxfordshire, and live bombing at Heligoland. Other tasks included a long-range mission undertaken to Dhahran in Saudi Arabia before the unit departed on 6 March. The 19th Bomb Squadron completed its TDY in February and was replaced by the 49th Bomb Squadron of the 2nd Bomb Group from Chatham Air Force Base, Georgia. The squadron was equipped with B-50As and three KB-29M tankers and commanded by Lieutenant Colonel George L. Newton Jr. The other two squadrons of the group were distributed between Marham and Lakenheath.

Life at the base could take a surprising turn as two airmen (it is not recorded whether these were RAF or USAF) were alleged to have stolen the station commander's car, which was later found abandoned upside down outside the camp. It was thought that an attempt had been made to dispose of some valuable, and possibly stolen, goods.

The eventual aim of a handover of the base to the USAF was beginning to cause anxiety among RAF personnel which was affecting morale. Airmen in married quarters were becoming uncertain about the future, and there were complaints about the alleged 'arrogance' of the US Base Complement Squadron, whose attitude was to 'alter all this when we take over'. RAF postings into the base were frozen, which caused problems for station routine, and there seemed to be a lack of decision-making from the top.[2]

Operational routine in April 1950 included Operation 'Stardust' on the 29th and 30th, in which the bombers carried out a fighter affiliation exercise with RAF Fighter Command. RAF personnel were also being trained on the B-29 Washingtons under the supervision of the crews of the 49th Bomb Squadron. One of these was Flight Sergeant W. Fairless of 115 Squadron based at Marham, a flight engineer on Halifaxes during the war, now posted to Sculthorpe as a 'pupil engineer' on the new aircraft. An entry in his logbook for April 1950 records a flight in a B-50 from 'Skulthorpe' [*sic*] to Heston for bombing practice. For the whole month his flying hours totalled five and a quarter. Later in June he was back at Marham completing a course in 'B-29 Cruise Control' under the supervision of USAF Air Training Command. During August he had amassed 66 hours' flying time in the Washington.[3]

The 49th Bomb Squadron left Sculthorpe on 20 May for Hunter Air Force Base in Georgia, one formation flying via Lagens in the Azores and the remainder via Keflavik in Iceland. Two squadrons of the 301st Bomb Group arrived from their base at Barksdale in Louisiana; the 352nd and 353rd Bomb Squadrons, the first commanded by Lieutenant Colonel Donald G. McPherson and the second by Major D. Richards. The third squadron, the 32nd, was placed at Lakenheath due to the RAF Washington units being at Marham. Squadron equipment consisted of B-29s and the KB-50M tankers.

At the end of May, RB-29s of the 72nd Strategic Reconnaissance Squadron, 5th Strategic Reconnaissance Wing, flew in from Fairfield-Suisun, California, under the command of Lieutenant Colonel Martin B. Schofield. Like the recently departed 23rd Strategic Reconnaissance Squadron, the 72nd was a sophisticated intelligence gathering unit whose aircraft were packed with the latest photographic and electronic equipment requiring 24/7 security at the base. This was a clandestine spy-plane unit whose central task was to patrol the periphery of the Iron Curtain countries around the Baltic and the Arctic regions eavesdropping on communications and attempting to identify military installations.

There was some decline in RAF personnel by May 1950, with 18 officers, 7 warrant officers, 25 senior NCOs and 256 corporals and airmen in post. The US Air Force complement numbered 94 officers and 1,007 enlisted men. There was still no firm decision about Sculthorpe's future status and constant complaints about the levels of RAF manning.

TRAGEDY STRIKES

Late in the afternoon of Wednesday 7 June 1950, RB-29A Superfortress 42-94081 of the 72nd Strategic Reconnaissance Squadron, with pilot Captain Henry J. Walsh and ten crew, took off from Sculthorpe on an air test and routine gunnery exercise over the North Sea. At around 700ft over the Dogger Bank area, a burst of gunfire from the forward upper gun turret hit No. 4 engine (the starboard outer) and it caught fire. The pilot was unable to maintain control and with the aircraft losing height the order was given for the crew to bail out at about 500ft. Eight crewmen jumped, but within minutes the aircraft had ditched in the sea 20 miles east of Cromer and broke up with three crew still aboard, including the captain, the tail gunner, Staff Sergeant Warren J. Ebert, and the radar observer, Captain Ladislow Vessel.

Captain Walsh and Sergeant Ebert managed to reach a dinghy safely but Captain Vessel died in the process. Later, the survivors were picked up by a Lowestoft trawler and the search for the remaining crewmen started. The Aldeburgh lifeboat was alerted along with aircraft from Sculthorpe, Mildenhall and Lakenheath. Over the next two days, RAF Lincolns and Ansons, USAF helicopters from the 7th Air Sea Rescue Squadron based at Wiesbaden in Germany, SB-29s with lifeboats, B-17s, C-47s and other aircraft with specialised equipment scoured the sea for the remaining survivors. A total of seven crew perished in the accident.

An additional concern was the loss of secret equipment aboard the aircraft. Wartime-level security was imposed at Great Yarmouth and Lowestoft quaysides when survivors were brought ashore and photographs were banned 'at the request of the American authorities'. There was obviously concern about how the news would be presented to next of kin and, not least, about the fate of the highly classified electronic equipment aboard the aircraft. The *Eastern Daily Press* of Saturday 10 June carried an interview with Captain Walsh, which included a tribute to the rescuers and a brief factual account of the events.

NEW CRISIS AND BASE HANDOVER TO USAF

The invasion by communist North Korea of South Korea on 25 June 1950 created one of the worst crises yet seen in the Cold War. Under the banner of the United Nations, the Western Allies were pledged to offer all military assistance to beleaguered South Korea, and there were fears that the Soviets might take advantage of the situation in Europe. Accordingly, the Americans requested that their bomber units in the UK be reinforced without delay. This required the bases at Mildenhall, Lakenheath and Sculthorpe to be brought to full strength and others to be prepared for active use, including Brize Norton, Fairford and Upper Heyford. This was no time to delay.

At Sculthorpe on 11 July, the two squadrons of the 301st Bomb Group left for Lakenheath, and at about the same time the 72nd Strategic Reconnaissance Squadron departed for Marham, later moving on to Burtonwood. This made way for the 97th Bomb Wing (Medium) headquarters, with the B-50Ds of the 97th Bomb Group's three squadrons, the 340th, 341st and 342nd. From their home base at Biggs in Texas, via Goose Bay, the first aircraft arrived on 15 July, with the remainder completing the trip by the 17th. Over the next few months there were detachments of the three squadrons to Wyton, Waddington, Oakington and Valley.

July 1950 saw a formidable increase in station strength at Sculthorpe which brought it to a level last seen in wartime. Group Captain H.C. Parker remained as station commanding officer. Brigadier General D.W. Hutchinson commanded 97th Bomb Wing, with the 97th Bomb Group commander Colonel D.E. Bailey. The 7502nd Air Support Group (later Wing) was commanded by Lieutenant Colonel C.L. Wimberly.

Increased security was much in evidence to guard against genuine fears of infiltration and sabotage. Nothing was left to chance. Army units for ground defence consisted of the 2nd Battalion of the Gloucestershire Regiment commanded by Lieutenant Colonel James P. Carne. Colonel Carne was later to make history leading 'the Glorious Glosters' at the Battle of the Imjin River in Korea in April 1951, being awarded the Victoria Cross and the Distinguished Service Order for his courage and endurance both in that battle and subsequently as a prisoner of war. The 4th Regiment of the Royal Horse Artillery was an additional unit posted in to strengthen station defences.

Anti-aircraft defences were provided by 43 Light Anti-Aircraft Regiment, Royal Artillery, commanded by Lieutenant Colonel Foster DSO, and 35 Light Anti-Aircraft Regiment, commanded by Lieutenant Colonel S.S. Fielden.

The numerical strength of the station in July stood at 18 RAF officers and just over 400 RAF NCOs and junior ranks. US Air Force personnel amounted to 326 officers and over 1,500 enlisted airmen. There were, in addition, 37 Army officers and over 600 soldiers, many of whom had to be accommodated in tented camps.

As discussions continued at the top levels of the US and British governments as to what bases were to accommodate the increased USAF forces within the UK, for Sculthorpe it was a question of not if but when the final handover would take place. It was an unsettling time for the RAF contingent and there was evidence of increasing friction with the Americans, in particular with the permanent USAF administrative unit, the 7502nd Air Support Wing. Group Captain Parker complained in his monthly report that orders issued by the RAF were being disregarded and in some cases 'the RAF station commander is denied access to his own station'.[4] Various station buildings were being handed over to USAF control, including the MT (Motor Transport) hangar, the Sergeants' Mess and the NAAFI Club. Liaison was breaking down, with consequent damage to morale, and in a few instances there were complaints that the Americans were behaving in an overbearing and even threatening manner. There seemed to be no agreement as to what had to be handed over to US control, and as late as November 1950 there was still no defined policy for a smooth transition of responsibilities.[5]

Airfield developments continued without delay to equip the base for the latest generation of heavy bombers, in particular the B-50 and the B-36 Peacemaker types. New hardstandings had to be constructed and existing ones repaired or extended, the aim being to make way for at least twelve B-36 bombers and anything up to twenty B-50s. There also had to be a sufficient overlap (at least 600ft) at either end of the main runway in the event of an aircraft overshooting. Other changes had important implications for the local community, not least in the rerouting of public roads surrounding the base (see Chapter Sixteen).

In the meantime, station life continued throughout the summer and autumn. The B-50s trained hard alongside the KB-29 tankers with in-flight refuelling equipment which extended their capabilities to strike at the western USSR should war become

The B-50D bomber. Note the additional front turret and external fuel tanks of the D variant.

a reality. September saw a succession of VIP visitors to the station, including Field Marshal Sir William Slim, the famous commander of the wartime Burma campaign, Lieutenant General James Doolittle, the airman who had led the first retaliatory attack on Tokyo in 1942, and the commanding general of the Third Air Division, Major General Johnson.

Preparations for final handover to the USAF of Lakenheath, Mildenhall and Sculthorpe proceeded. With winter approaching, it was clear that not all personnel could be billeted on the bases at any one time, and therefore civilian accommodation would be required, not easy at a time of housing shortage for local people – for Sculthorpe the estimate was that at least 700 men would have to live off base in the local community.

By the end of the year most of the airfield functions had been handed over to USAF responsibility and the necessary training completed, including air traffic control, signals, armaments, crash and fire and the oxygen replenishment sections. By the end of January, the station sick quarters were handed over and preparations were being made for the final withdrawal of the RAF contingent to Bircham Newton, except for a few liaison officers.

The handing-over ceremony took place on 1 February 1951 by No. 3 Group RAF Bomber Command to the Third Air Division. The RAF ensign was lowered in the presence of Wing Commander W.L. Jones DFC, Colonel H.C. Dorney, commander of the 97th Bomb Wing, and Colonel T.G. Corhin, commander of the 7502nd Air Support Wing. Colonel Corhin took temporary command of the station in place of Brigadier General D.W. Hutchinson.

As with Lakenheath and other stations handed over to the Americans, the RAF designation was retained, as were RAF liaison officers. A new era had arrived at Sculthorpe, full of possibilities but with all the uncertainties and dangers that existed at the height of the Cold War.

NOTES

1. AIR 28/1110 Operations Record Book: RAF Sculthorpe, 1949–51.
2. Ibid.
3. Extracted from Logbook of Flt Sgt W. Fairless, RAF, RAF Museum, Hendon.
4. AIR 28/1110.
5. Ibid.

7. AIRFIELD AND USAF EXPANSION

'There was always an 'A' bomb aboard and a target in Russia if we got the order when airborne within a certain distance from Russia.'

(Wing Commander Ken Wallis on flying the B-36 Peacemaker)

Sculthorpe was a small cog in the very large wheel of the US Air Force presence in Britain by the early 1950s. Plans had been drawn up to allocate at least thirty-four airfields for USAF use, at least half of them former RAF satellite stations which had seen very little use.

In order to match the growing size and strength of USAF units in Britain, two important changes took place within the command structure. Firstly, the 7th Air Division was formed in March 1951 to take responsibility for all Strategic Air Command (SAC) bomber and fighter units visiting the UK on a rotational basis, with headquarters at South Ruislip. Brigadier General Paul T. Cullen was appointed its first commander and set out for England on 23 March, accompanied by over fifty USAF staff in a giant Douglas C-124A Globemaster. Over the North Atlantic, the aircraft suffered a catastrophic failure and no trace of the aircraft or personnel were ever found, in spite of a search by over 100 aircraft and several surface ships including the carrier *Coral Sea*. Major General Archie J. Old Jr. was then given temporary command until he was, in turn, succeeded by Major General John P. McConnell on 24 May.

During the same month, the Third Air Division was raised to the status of the Third Air Force, also with headquarters at South Ruislip and now part of the United States Air Forces Europe (USAFE) and commanded by Major General Leon W. Johnson. The new command added tactical units to its responsibilities based at Mildenhall, Lakenheath, Sculthorpe, Wyton and Bassingbourn, and fighter jets at Manston in Kent. The task was to support the logistical element of the USAF in the UK and to conduct training and operations in support of NATO.

As the work of the Third Air Force expanded, the 49th Air Division was activated in October 1951 to supervise and control operations with headquarters at Sculthorpe

USAF at Sculthorpe. Station sign on display in the Norfolk and Suffolk Aviation Museum, Flixton. (Norfolk and Suffolk Aviation Museum)

from 1 June 1952 to 1 July 1956. Its component parts were the 47th Bombardment Wing (at Sculthorpe – more will be said about this unit later) and the 20th Fighter-Bomber Wing (FBW) based at Wethersfield in Essex and Woodbridge in Suffolk. Thus much of the structure that was to endure in the early part of the Cold War was established by the end of 1951.[1]

NUCLEAR STRIKE CAPABILITY

One of the factors complicating the relations between the United States and Britain over nuclear matters throughout this period was the existence of the McMahon Act (Atomic Energy Act) passed by the US Congress in August 1946, which prohibited the passing of information or help on atomic matters to any other nation (see Chapter Four). This of course included Britain and the news was received in government circles with some shock. For many years the Act's existence resulted in much unease about American policy with regard to nuclear weapons on British soil – it was not until 1958 that the Americans amended the policy in favour of the UK.

The Boeing B-50 was fully capable of carrying nuclear weapons and during 1950 some arrived carrying such weapons, but with nuclear cores separate and possibly retained within the United States, although the details about this are obviously obscure. It would seem surprising if American bombers were operating from the UK relying on conventional bombs alone and without access to nuclear weapons or the possibility of obtaining them. But preparations were being made for a US nuclear stockpile within certain UK bases. As early as 1946 an article in *The Washington Post* of 10 October had stated that atomic bombs were being stockpiled in Britain – a claim denied by President Truman. What is clear is that as early as 1948 some British bases were 'atomic capable', or equipped for the storage of nuclear weapons, including Sculthorpe. Non-nuclear components of the bombs were being stored in some British bases by the end of July 1950.[2]

A number of aviation field depot squadrons were assigned to various bombardment wings, many stationed at British bases, whose purpose was 'the assembly, maintenance and loading of the atomic/nuclear weapons (or 'Special Weapons' as they were called – the Mark 5 Atomic Bomb) [...] and assuring the weapons training level of key flight crew personnel within the combat units'.[3]

These units had been trained at Sandia Base, Albuquerque, New Mexico towards the end of 1950, before being assigned to active duty, mostly in the European theatre.

Within the UK, the aviation field depot squadrons were distributed as follows: the 1st Aviation Field Depot Squadron (AFDS) at Upper Heyford (1951–58), the 2nd at Fairford (1951–56), the 4th at Greenham Common (1955–64) and the 8th at Lakenheath (from 1951 and at intervals until 1959).[4] In addition, the 9th AFDS was known to be present at Sculthorpe from March 1953 until being absorbed into the 1st Tactical Depot Squadron (TDS) in June 1954, the latter unit having been present at Sculthorpe as the 1st Tactical Support Squadron (TSS) since April 1952.

Needless to say, these assignment movements were highly classified at the time, and no less so than at Sculthorpe. The 1st Tactical Support Squadron had a different label but the same background training and role as any of the aviation field depot squadrons. The 1st TSS had been assigned in great secrecy to Sculthorpe in April 1952, in advance of the 47th Bomb Wing. Two sections of the unit were flown in advance by air to make preparations, and a third section made the journey by troopship. There was some surprise when a national magazine carried a long article about the unit movement, and on arrival at Southampton in England, the personnel were greeted by large banners reading 'HUSBANDS WANTED'. Within hours it was alleged that 'Moscow Molly', greeted their arrival by radio – so much for the secrecy! The welcome at Sculthorpe was fairly low-key, with only one British officer present to hand the base over to them.[5]

When the 9th AFDS arrived at Sculthorpe in March of the following year there were two units present, basically carrying out the same task. The personnel knew each other socially but no questions were asked. By June 1954, the 9th AFDS was absorbed within the 1st Tactical Depot Squadron (TDS) as explained above. Some of the security personnel were assigned to the Air Police Squadron. Eight detachments were formed from the new unit: Detachment 1 at Wethersfield, Det. 2 at Bentwaters, Det. 3 remaining at Sculthorpe, Det. 4 at Manston, Det. 5 at Woodbridge, Det. 6 also at Wethersfield, Det. 7 at Alconbury and Det. 8 at Shepherds Grove.[6]

The infrastructure at the bases included 'Special Ammunition Stores', exclusively for the storage of nuclear weapons and possibly also nerve gas (in some cases) – hardened shelters built of thick concrete with guard towers, floodlit at night with high double fences and guard dogs on the loose within the perimeter.[7] During 1956, new bomb stores were constructed on the north-east side of Sculthorpe to replace the former structures on the south-west side. Between 1956 and 1958 the old bomb dump on the south-west was closed.

Making preparations for a nuclear stockpile was not the same thing as possessing one but, prompted by public opinion, the British government had to ensure that the United States would not use atomic weapons from British soil without UK government consent. The question of nuclear weapons was often a game of bluff and counterbluff – it suited the Americans to keep the Soviet Union guessing about our capability. In the meantime, Britain was developing its own nuclear weaponry, having tested an atomic bomb in October 1952 and bringing into service its first nuclear bomb, named the 'Blue Danube', in 1953.[8] The other factor to consider was that in any forthcoming war (during the early 1950s at least) it was doubtful if the Soviets had any reliable means of delivering atomic weapons – which is why aerial reconnaissance played such a vital role during these years (see account of the Secret Flights in Chapter 8).

ARRIVAL OF THE B-36 'PEACEMAKER'

A fresh spectacle appeared in the skies over Lakenheath in January 1951, the sight of the sensational Convair B-36 'Peacemaker', the latest and yet most formidable bomber in the armoury of Strategic Air Command. These aircraft from the 7th Bomb Wing were on a brief visit to some of the East Anglian bases, including Sculthorpe, although at this time there were no plans to place the aircraft over here on a more permanent basis, partly because of the massive infrastructure required to service and maintain them on base. It did no harm to showcase around the world the hardware available to Strategic Air Command.

Convair B-36 Peacemaker. (Green Park Centre, Sculthorpe)

The aircraft had entered service with the US Air Force in 1948 and was reputed to be the largest bomber in the world, powered by six piston engines backed by four turbojets, which gave it a truly global range of 8,000 to 9,000 miles at a maximum height of well over 40,000ft. With a crew of twenty-two, the aircraft had a battery of 16 x 20mm cannon and endurance for over 45 hours in the air, and cruising speed of around 290mph. Verrall Grimes recalled the awesome sight of the B-36 bombers at Sculthorpe from the vantage point of his work in the NCO Club at the base: 'I remember the very long runway and the huge B-36 bombers, six pusher airscrews, twin jets on wing tips and ten engines with very high tails.'

Tony Nelson was a schoolboy in North Creake with an avid interest in the comings and goings at Sculthorpe, which on rare occasions would include the 'grand-daddy' of them all, the B-36 'Peacemaker', which could be heard from miles away – 'what a wonderful sight and sound'.

One major concern was the vulnerability of piston-engined bombers in the face of jet fighter attack – one lesson learned from the experiences of the B-29 crews in Korea, who had been easy prey for the marauding Chinese MiG-15s – hence the new emphasis in SAC on the need for long-range fighter escorts. It was also known that the Russians had improved their radar and anti-aircraft capability, which they had been able to evaluate in the Korean theatre of war. But, in spite of these problems, the B-36 was to remain the backbone of SAC for several years until the B-47 and B-52 jet bombers were fully deployed. Wing Commander Ken Wallis recalled his experience of the B-36 during a two-year exchange posting with Strategic Air Command in 1956, and his encounters with its legendary, tough commander, Lieutenant General Curtis LeMay:

My post in SAC HQ was in Armament (Electronics) but Curt Le May[9] once said to me 'You can fly, can't you?' I replied that I could since I had converted to Meteors and Vampires. He asked me if I would like to take part in some SAC exercises. That is how I became one of the four pilots in a crew of 22, flying the giant Convair RB-36H. There was always an 'A' bomb aboard and a target in Russia if we got the order when airborne within a certain distance from Russia, over the North Pole or off the coast while over the Bering Sea. The flight generally took about 30 hours with landings at Burtonwood or Greenham Common in the UK or Yokota in Japan.

As Ken looked through a window in the pressurised tunnel behind the cockpit area it was possible to see the 'A' Bomb at the ready: 'It was a great relief not to get the order to use it ...'[10]

After retiring from the RAF, Ken undertook pioneering work with the autogyro as an engineer and test pilot. A memorable event for him was his part in the James Bond film *You Only Live Twice*, when he acted as Bond's double in an aerial combat sequence, flying the autogyro 'Little Nellie', which he had built himself.

The 97th Bomb Group had vacated Sculthorpe in February 1951. There was a brief deployment of the B-36 during November 1951. During that month, the B-29s of the 19th Bomb Squadron, 22nd Bomb Wing, arrived bearing some bomb symbols earned during their recent service in the Korean War. This turned out to be the last SAC bomber unit to be deployed at Sculthorpe.

Earlier in the year, the arrival of the 91st Strategic Reconnaissance Wing with the latest RB-45 jets had signalled a fresh and more clandestine role for the base.

NOTES

1. Jackson, R.J.: *Strike Force: The USAF in Britain since 1948,* pp.42–44.
2. Young, Prof. Ken: 'US atomic capability and the British forward bases in the Cold War', *Journal of Contemporary History* 42(1), Jan. 2007, pp.117–36.
3. Lloyd, Alwyn T.: *A Cold War Legacy: A Tribute to Strategic Air Command 1946–1992,* pp.124–5.
4. Ibid.
5. Extract from www.usafnukes.com.
6. Ibid.
7. Campbell, Duncan, *The Unsinkable Aircraft Carrier: American Military Power in Britain,* pp.41–42.
8. 'Blue Danube' bombs were stored in bunkers at Barnham, Suffolk, and Faldingworth, Lincolnshire.
9. The film *Dr Strangelove* portrays a war-mad general who is a thinly disguised Gen. Curtis LeMay.
10. Letter from W/Cdr K.H. Wallis to author, 18 Feb. 2012.

8. SECRET FLIGHTS

'More secret than the Manhattan Project ...'

(Squadron Leader John Crampton)

A NEW AIRCRAFT AND A FRESH ROLE

By January 1951, Norfolk people must have become inured to the sights and sounds of unusual aircraft plying the skies but there was yet another surprise in store: the North American RB-45C Tornado, the first four-engined operational jet to be seen in Europe.

Arriving at Manston in January 1951, the first four RB-45C Tornados were accompanied by four KB-29 tankers which together made up the first detachment of the 323rd Strategic Reconnaissance Squadron (SRS), 91st Strategic Reconnaissance Wing (SRW) from Barksdale Air Force Base in Louisiana. The RB-45, the reconnaissance variant of the B-45 bomber, predated Britain's first jet bomber, the English Electric Canberra, which entered service with 101 Squadron a few months later in May 1951.

The B-45 had first flown in 1947 and entered service a year later as a tactical light bomber, the first of the USAF jet bombers, capable of carrying nuclear as well as conventional bombs. The RB-45C had been developed as a high-altitude reconnaissance aircraft and the first batch were delivered to Strategic Air Command in 1948. The crew of four consisted of a pilot, co-pilot/radio operator, photo-navigator and tail gunner, although the latter could be replaced by a pair of .50 calibre fixed machine guns. Towards the end of 1950 and early 1951 the aircraft saw their baptism of fire in Korea when they were tasked with flying reconnaissance missions along the Manchurian–Korean border. For several months they survived unscathed, running the gauntlet of the communist MiG-15 fighters, although one aircraft failed to return from a mission of 4 December 1950. By the following spring, experience dictated that the aircraft should operate at night, under cover of darkness, as the best hope of avoiding detection and interception.

Within days of touching down at Manston, the 323rd Squadron detachment moved to Sculthorpe as part of the plan to rotate units of the 91st Wing for three-month assignments in the UK. The remaining components of the wing were at Lockbourne, Ohio, and Yokota in Japan.

SPIES IN THE SKY AND WESTERN INTELLIGENCE

The 91st SRW at Sculthorpe resumed the role carried out in Korea – aerial photore-connaissance, mapping and electronic intelligence gathering (ELINT). One of the tasks was to undertake detailed photoreconnaissance mapping of the Rhine river, between the English Channel and Switzerland, to provide NATO forces with knowledge of the terrain they would be fighting over in the event of a Soviet invasion of Europe. Missions would be flown over Europe on a daily basis lasting about 10 hours, with refuelling by a KB-29 tanker of 6,000 gallons before returning to base. There were strict instructions to avoid drifting into heavily defended Soviet-controlled airspace, as harsh lessons had been learned about the dangers of daylight overflights of enemy territory in Korea. Yet since the outbreak of the Korean War, there were fears in the intelligence community that the Soviets might attempt a surprise nuclear attack in Europe, possibly even by smuggling an atomic bomb into Britain and detonating it in a densely populated area or by mounting a suicide bombing mission.[1]

There had been a serious deficit of hard intelligence about the Soviet Union and its allies since the onset of the Cold War, and the contrast could hardly have been greater with the experience of the Second World War, when the ULTRA system enabled the allies to break the secret codes of enemy communications. However, since 1940 there had been one vital breakthrough which arose from SIGINT (signals intelligence) and was given the code name VENONA, a secret which was even hidden from the American President Franklin Roosevelt, and for some years from Harry Truman. VENONA decrypts were shared by the Americans with the British and what they revealed was the extent of Soviet infiltration into the heart of Western intelligence agencies. The problem was that VENONA decrypts still left many gaps in information gathering, especially as far as British intelligence was concerned, and, according to MI5 historian Christopher Andrew, failed for many years to reveal the identities of 'the ablest group of British agents ever recruited by a foreign power' – the so-called 'Cambridge Five' – Kim Philby, Guy Burgess, Donald Maclean, Anthony Blunt and John Cairncross, all recruited at or just after leaving Cambridge University in the mid-1930s.[2] All were products of the top English public schools before going up to Cambridge, Maclean's alma mater being Gresham's School in Holt, Norfolk. The authorities were aware of an inner ring of spies but it took seven years before a partial VENONA decrypt revealed the identity of the first of the 'Five' in 1951, Donald Maclean. Not until 1974 was Blunt identified and the last of the 'Five', John Cairncross, unmasked as late as 1982.[3]

In spite of VENONA, according to Christopher Andrew, 'the transition from war to Cold War brought with it a transition from intelligence feast to intelligence famine'.[4] The advantage lay with the other side, as dedicated Soviet agents had infiltrated some of the inner circles of Western intelligence agencies. As early as 1941, Klaus Fuchs, a German–British national, had begun to pass on the secrets of the Manhattan Project to the Soviets, which enabled them to design an atomic bomb which was almost an exact copy of the American version. Fuchs was able to operate until he was finally unmasked and convicted in 1950.

The Soviet Union and its satellite countries operated as closed societies where news management and daily life were controlled by the state backed by secret police. There were few if any reliable Western agents at work and it was only by the 1970s and 1980s that a series of defections from behind the Iron Curtain began to reveal any hard facts. The contrast between this and the comparative openness of the Western way of life could hardly have been greater, with the freedom of the media to report basic facts about military and aviation movements, bases and installations. Indeed, so anxious were the American and British governments to keep public opinion on side that it became the fashion to hold a series of airfield 'open days' to showcase the latest British and American aircraft. But there were strict limits over nuclear issues and other sensitive activities.

ORIGINS OF THE OVERFLIGHTS

In the absence of hard intelligence about Soviet military installations and force dispositions, there seemed only one remaining option: aerial reconnaissance. Years before the existence of satellite imagery and aerial 'drones' (unmanned aircraft), aerial photography and reconnaissance by manned aircraft had proved their worth in war and peace. Indeed the pedigree of such activity predates the First World War, and even provided the motive for aircraft being adopted by the military in the first place. During the Second World War, the high-flying Spitfires of the photoreconnaissance (PRU) units almost became a legend, but during the Cold War aerial reconnaissance was to take on a more sinister and dangerous aspect in which Sculthorpe was to play a leading role.

It was never going to be sufficient to rely on reconnaissance flights around the perimeter of the Soviet territories, however sophisticated the electronic monitoring might be. There were many unanswered questions about the threat posed by the Soviet Union. Strategic Air Command needed to know about the locations and extent of Soviet defences, radar and other installations, airfields and other possible targets in a future war. Not only did Russia possess the atomic bomb but was also known to be developing the means to deliver it in the Tupolev Tu4 bomber (NATO code name *Bull*), which had first flown in 1947 and began to enter service in 1949. Incidentally, this aircraft was almost an exact copy of the American Boeing B-29, an example of which had fallen into Russian hands towards the end of the war. It was feared that this aircraft would have the capability to deliver nuclear weapons as far as the American mainland. The question was: how many bombers did the Soviets possess, and where were they based?

Thus, as early as 1946, US aircraft from the 46th Strategic Reconnaissance Squadron were overflying Alaska and the northern Soviet Union on reconnaissance missions. A few such missions were being flown throughout the later 1940s and during the Korean War; both the RAF and USAF were flying electronic intelligence (ELINT) missions monitoring radar and other communications around the Soviet and Chinese borders. The first known casualty of a spy flight occurred on 8 April 1950 when a US Navy PB4Y-2 Privateer flying from its base in Morocco was shot down by Soviet La-11 fighters over the Baltic Sea, bordering the Latvian coast. The task had been to eavesdrop on the Soviet fleet but the Americans always claimed the incident had taken place over international waters. All the crew were lost.

At this point President Harry Truman took the step of banning overflights pending a full review, as he felt the risks were too great with the Korean War at its height.[5] However, General LeMay and US defence chiefs were desperate for the sort of intelligence that could only be obtained by overflights of Soviet territory, and at this point the spotlight shifted to the so-called 'special relationship' with the UK government. Prime Minister Clement Attlee had been alarmed by the US threat to use the atomic bomb if the situation in Korea got out of hand, fearing that this might put Britain directly in the path of a European nuclear war. Accordingly, he flew to the United States towards the end of 1950 to confer with President Truman, to secure some assurance that the US would not use the bomb without consulting the British government in advance. Truman stopped short of accepting a British veto over the use of the atomic bomb, instead agreeing to 'inform' the UK government if such circumstances arose. There then followed a sort of diplomatic trade-off whereby Britain agreed to back US policy 100 per cent in Europe and the Far East, to stand shoulder to shoulder in the face of aggression and to strengthen and maintain defences. At the same time, it was agreed that Britain would 'join the United States in co-ordinated periodic overflights of the Soviet Union to locate the air bases and dispositions of its long-range bomber forces that could conduct surprise atomic attacks on the west'.[6] The intelligence resulting from such flights would be shared between the US and the UK.

The Royal Air Force definitely had the will for such an enterprise but lacked the means. Relying on wartime vintage Mosquitoes, Avro Lancasters and Lincolns, the RAF had carried out a number of reconnaissance flights on the fringes of Soviet airspace. There is also some anecdotal evidence that the RAF had mounted penetration flights over Soviet territory, setting out from bases like Fayid in the Suez Canal zone and Habbaniya in Iraq. No. 13 PR Squadron based at Fayid had operated their

Mosquito PR34s – a very long-range version of the earlier PR16 – on such missions in 1948.[7] But these aircraft were clearly inadequate for this more ambitious task. The answer was for the RAF to employ American aircraft like the RB-45, but with British markings. The obvious advantage of this plan for the Americans was that they could deny responsibility in the event of an aircraft being shot down over Soviet territory.

Thus, a new unit was formed and the attention shifted to Sculthorpe, in what became one of the most intriguing and, until recent years, most closely guarded secrets of the Cold War.

RAF SPECIAL DUTY FLIGHT AND OPERATION 'JU-JITSU'

In mid-1951 the RAF Special Duty Flight was formed at Sculthorpe alongside the 323rd Strategic Reconnaissance Squadron of the 91st Strategic Reconnaissance Wing. Three RB-45C aircraft were to be transferred to the unit, a type already being operated by the American squadron. These aircraft had an in-flight refuelling capacity which enabled them to extend their range and were capable of flying at Mach 0.72 (about 550mph) up to a height of around 38,000ft, supposedly well beyond the ceiling of Soviet fighters. The first choice of a commander was Squadron Leader Micky Martin, of Dambusters fame,[8] but he failed in the decompression testing. Another leader was found in Squadron Leader John Crampton, experienced both in Bomber Command operations and in jet flying. Nicknamed 'Big John', at 6ft 6in in height, he was one of the RAF's tallest pilots and had been awarded the Distinguished Flying Cross (DFC) serving with Halifaxes on No. 76 Squadron during the war. In July 1951 he was commanding No. 97 Squadron at Hemswell, flying Lincolns, describing himself at the time as a 'happy boss'. He was a lover of fast cars, like the Grand Prix Maserati he brought with him to Sculthorpe. This was an interest he was to share with his friend Ken Wallis, who met him after the Sculthorpe episode and remained friends with him in later life.

Crampton was summoned to a meeting with the AOC-in-C Bomber Command Air Chief Marshal Sir Hugh Pughe Lloyd, or 'Huff Puff' in RAF parlance, to be told of his new appointment with the Special Duty Flight but nothing was revealed about the forthcoming operation at this stage, which was a carefully guarded secret. Eight crews, each comprising two pilots and a navigator from various RAF squadrons, were posted to Sculthorpe and almost immediately were flown out to Barksdale Air Force Base in Louisiana for an introduction to the RB-45C. Further training continued at Langley AFB in Virginia and Lockbourne AFB in Ohio. On one occasion at Lockbourne, an unfortunate RAF pilot made a heavy landing at night, writing off the aircraft but not injuring the crew. The result was a stormy interview for the offender with General Curtis LeMay at SAC headquarters in Omaha, Nebraska, and the premature departure of the pilot for England.

RB-45 in-flight refuelling. (Paul Lashmar)

RAF aircrew with USAF officer at Sculthorpe. Sqn Ldr Crampton back row third from left, *c.* 1952. (Paul Lashmar)

The conversion course was completed by the end of the year and the RAF aircrews returned to Sculthorpe for further training with the USAF, including in-flight refuelling and practice day and night using cameras and radar. At this point, none of the crews knew what they were being trained for and speculation was rife – one slight complication being the fact that the RAF personnel included three NCOs who were billeted in the enlisted men's quarters, increasing the chance of a security leak, although there was also intense curiosity about the RAF unit in the American officers' club. The appointment of a USAF liaison officer, Lieutenant Colonel Marion 'Hack' Mixson, in early 1952 did much to ease the situation.

In the meantime there had been changes at the highest level of government, with the return of Winston Churchill as prime minister in the general election of October 1951. Almost immediately, Churchill had flown to Washington DC to confer with President Truman and managed to secure an agreement about the use of atomic weapons from British bases which appeared to provide more safeguards than those which had been negotiated by Attlee. In the case of US air bases in England 'in an emergency', any atomic attack against the Soviet Union would have to be a matter for 'joint decision' by both governments. Shortly after his return to England on 24 February 1952, Churchill penned a note to the Secretary of State for Air approving the RAF overflight of the Soviet Union. Headed 'Most Secret', the note continued, 'Operation Ju Jitsu will be done by us if the Americans cannot be pursuaded [sic] to do it. I am to be informed at least a week before it happens.'[9]

Crampton was again summoned to RAF Bomber Command headquarters at High Wycombe, accompanied by his navigator Flight Lieutenant Rex Sanders, to be told that their mission was to undertake deep penetration radar reconnaissance over the Soviet Union, in three tracks; one from Sculthorpe to the Baltic states, the second to the Moscow area and the third towards southern Russia. The mission was to be flown at night as radar reconnaissance, unlike photo reconnaissance, did not require light. There would be a link-up with KB-29 tankers for aerial refuelling just to the north of Denmark. The objectives were to track some of the routes marked out for RAF and SAC bombers in the event of war, to test Soviet air defences, and in particular to gather intelligence on Soviet surface-to-air missiles, which were known to be in the process of development. Needless to say at this stage absolute secrecy was paramount and, as Squadron Leader Crampton admitted, the whole enterprise was 'more secret than the Manhattan Project'.

FIRST FLIGHT

Although the actual date of the flight had not yet been fixed, the crews were briefed at Sculthorpe and the news was greeted with some shock. None of the aircrew were volunteers and many were hardened veterans of the bomber campaign over Germany who, by now, had reason to hope that they had done their bit. A typical reaction was 'What have they let us in for? Why us?' from a man who had survived fifty operations over Germany. For one pilot enough was enough and he decided to withdraw from the enterprise and return to his unit, with all the possible consequences that security might be jeopardised.

Four aircraft were available, one as a spare. Two of the RB-45s were flown to West Raynham to a secure hangar where all traces of USAF markings were stripped off and RAF roundels painted on, something which must have aroused some curiosity at West Raynham. In early March, Squadron Leader Crampton with his crew, Flight Lieutenant Sanders and Flight Sergeant Joe Acklam, had flown a probing mission over the Soviet zone of East Germany, fast and at maximum height, to monitor the reactions of defences. There was nothing of any consequence to report.

On 16 April the final details of the mission were revealed to Crampton and Sanders at High Wycombe when the three routes were marked out on the wall map. For use in the event of being shot down and captured, elaborate cover stories were concocted, accompanied by false flight plans and maps, to try to convince the Soviets that the aircraft had got lost. The purpose of the RAF roundels was to enable the Americans to deny all knowledge of the flight and the British to claim that they did not employ this aircraft type. All this assumed a level of gullibility among the Soviets that was hard to believe. The consequences of an aircraft being shot down would have been dire, both for the crews concerned and for possible international repercussions. It could have been seen as an act of war and at the very

RB-45s with RAF roundels but no serials, Sculthorpe. Note large fin tip-tanks. (Paul Lashmar)

least cause the downfall of the Churchill government. The Soviets had been aware of previous attempts to overfly their territory but were reluctant to expose publicly the inadequacy of their defence systems.

Late in the afternoon of 17 April the three aircraft took off, the first crew being Squadron Leader Crampton, Flight Lieutenant Sanders and Sergeant Bill Lindsay. The second crew consisted of Flight Lieutenant Gordon Cremer, Flight Sergeant Bob Anstee and Sergeant Don Greenslade. Flight Lieutenants Bill Blair, John Hill and Flight Sergeant Joe Acklam made up the third crew.

The aircraft made for the Skagerrak dividing Denmark and Sweden, located the tankers to take on a maximum fuel load, and then headed for Soviet airspace at 36,000ft, with no navigation lights and in total radio silence except for the OMG ('Oh My God') frequency in an extreme emergency. Crampton took the longest and most southerly route, south-east across Russia and the Ukraine at Mach 0.68 (about 520mph), covering around thirty potential targets in a 1,000-mile flight over hostile territory, with the crew photographing radar displays. He later remarked on the vast land area they flew over: he found the experience 'all so quiet and distinctly eerie'.[10] Of the other crews further north, one headed towards Germany and the Baltic states, and the second crew south of that route through Germany and towards Moscow.

After a flight lasting 10 hours, 20 minutes, Crampton and his crew returned safely to Sculthorpe after a second refuelling on their way out of Soviet airspace. The remaining two aircraft had completed their sorties but weather forced diversions to Manston and Copenhagen.

The overflights provided valuable information about the Soviet air defences and data about their long-range bomber force of Tu-4s and its locations. Targets for SAC in any future war could be more exactly pinpointed. The flights had been detected by the Soviets, who were enraged by this intrusion, and a commission was set up to investigate what had gone wrong.

In recognition of their success, Squadron Leader Crampton and his crews flew their aircraft to SAC headquarters in Omaha, Nebraska, for personal congratulations from General LeMay. On their return to England, Crampton was awarded the AFC (Air Force Cross) and the other crews received AFCs or AFMs. The AFC was a non-combatant decoration which required no citation, and therefore some were issued to aircrew as a result of secret intelligence work. After this it was business as usual as the crews were posted back to their units. Squadron Leader Crampton was appointed to command No. 101 Squadron at Binbrook, equipped with Canberras. He compared this aircraft to the RB-45 as being 'not unlike a Ford Escort after having given up a stretched Cadillac'.[11]

Four RB-45Cs in RAF roundels but no serials with RAF and USAF aircrews and groundcrews, c. 1952. (Paul Lashmar)

RB-45C with RAF and USAF crew, Sqn Ldr Crampton in centre, c. 1952. (Paul Lashmar)

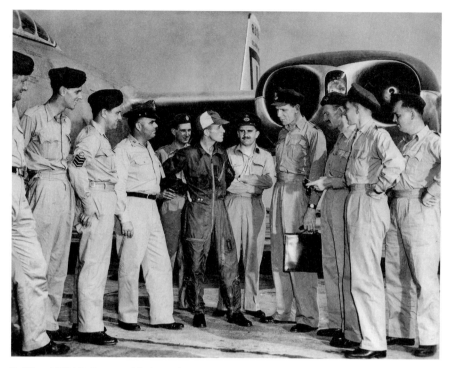

RAF and USAF aircrew with Sqn Ldr Crampton, fourth from right. (Paul Lashmar)

SECOND FLIGHT

Towards the end of 1952, a second RAF overflight was contemplated, presumably due to the success of the first. Dwight D. Eisenhower had just been elected President of the United States and there was no change in the presidential decision to ban over-flights, so once again US defence chiefs were looking to the RAF.

Crampton was once again summoned to High Wycombe. There were a few crew changes on his return to Sculthorpe but Colonel Mixson was there to welcome the RAF men back. Sergeant Bill Lindsay was replaced as Crampton's co-pilot by Flight Lieutenant Robert 'Mac' Furze, one of the No. 101 Squadron flight commanders. Another addition was Flight Lieutenant Harry Currell. Throughout November and December 1952 there was hard flight training but the mission was suddenly cancelled and the crews once again returned to their units. No clear reason for this has emerged, except that another overflight at this time over Russia may have been considered too great a risk. It has even been speculated that information had been leaked via Kim Philby or one of the 'Cambridge' spies. The four RB-45Cs were flown back to Lockbourne, Ohio, where their RAF markings raised a few eyebrows.[12]

In the meantime, much had changed. The resident unit at Sculthorpe since June 1952 had been the 47th Bombardment Wing, equipped with the B-45 and RB-45C, and the unit was destined for a long stay (see Chapter Nine). In the international arena, three nuclear tests towards the end of the year in eastern Kazakhstan testified to growing Soviet nuclear capability and there were reports of work on a replacement for the Tu-4 bomber, which indeed was the case as the Tu-16 *Badger* entered service in 1954. In addition, there was a missile range at Kapustin Yar, north of the Caspian Sea, where the Soviets were testing missiles based on the German V2 rockets, with the assistance of captured German scientists.

Apart from the Special Duty Flight at Sculthorpe, No. 192 Squadron based at Watton, and equipped with Lincolns, Washingtons and later Canberras, had been carrying out electronic surveillance in the Baltic area since 1951. In an attempt to gather information about Kapustin Yar, Project 'Robin' was launched, involving an overflight by a Royal Air Force Canberra to that area at a maximum height of up to 63,000ft (a record height reached earlier that year by a Canberra). Photographs were taken of the site but Soviet defences were alerted and the Canberra was lucky to land safely in Iran.

Thus, it was not surprising that the Special Duty Flight was reactivated in early 1954, once again at Sculthorpe. Squadron Leader Crampton was summoned to High Wycombe and found himself back at Sculthorpe in March, to be welcomed back by Colonel Mixson and to be greeted by 'the stretched Cadillacs, American flying clothing, American English and the raised eyebrows'.[13] But this time he was taken aback by what seemed to be a fairly open secret that something very special was about to happen, which could well have reached the ears even of the most bumbling Soviet spy or sympathiser. The RAF personnel had to maintain the fiction that they were ordinary exchange crews.

Once again there was a briefing session at Bomber Command headquarters at High Wycombe. Three routes were outlined: north, central and a very long southern track, the latter involving two refuelling rendezvous, on the way in and on the flight out. Needless to say, Squadron Leader Crampton chose the longest and most difficult route.

Back at Sculthorpe, four RB-45Cs were painted with RAF markings. There were two main mission objectives, to test and monitor Soviet air defences and to update information about Soviet bomber and missile bases. The preflight briefing was upbeat about the risks involved as it was anticipated that the RB-45s would be flying too high and fast to be in danger from either anti-aircraft fire (flak) or night fighters and any threat from SAMs (surface-to-air missiles) would be mitigated by the fact that they were unguided. While the flights were proceeding, GCHQ (Government Communications Headquarters) in Cheltenham would be eavesdropping on communications from the Soviet air defence network. Once again strict radio silence was to be maintained.

Late in the afternoon of 28 April the three RB-45s took off from Sculthorpe and headed for northern Denmark for the refuelling rendezvous and then into Soviet airspace to locate and photograph the designated targets from the radarscope.

John Crampton was surprised by a series of flashes visible from the ground and as they pressed on towards Kiev at a height of 36,000ft and around 530mph (Mach 0.7) it became obvious that the flashes were anti-aircraft bursts which were detonating at their height – they were being closely tracked by the air defences. In fact, the entire Soviet air defence network had been activated and it was later admitted by General Vladimir Abramov, commander of the Kiev region, that MiG pilots had been ordered to ram the intruding aircraft because the Russian fighters lacked radar. One of the pilots, Lieutenant Nikolai Sysoev, later interviewed for the BBC *Timewatch* programme *Spies in the Sky* (February 1994), stated that 'ideally we weren't meant to ram the plane head-on, but to ram the most vulnerable parts'.

Having taken evasive action, Crampton decided to steer a course for West Germany, still 1,000 miles away. He considered the option of jettisoning the now empty 1,200-gallon wing tanks to supply extra speed but realised that this would betray more details about the origins of the flight and General LeMay would be less than impressed if US Air Force hardware were to be scattered around the Russian countryside. By the time they reached the West German border they were unable to link up with the refuelling tanker owing to an equipment failure, and instead landed at Fürstenfeldbruck without further incident after 11 hours in the air. The next day they flew back to Sculthorpe where they met up with the other crews who had not faced any opposition in their flights.

AFTERMATH

For this second daring feat, Squadron Leader Crampton was awarded a bar to his AFC. The photographs and information collected provided valuable information at a critical period about Soviet military targets, their exact location and extent. But the risks were so great that no further RAF overflights were attempted, as far as is known, and certainly none from Sculthorpe. But that did not apply to the Americans, who carried out another similar flight from Sculthorpe on 29 March 1955. Three RB-45Cs from the 19th Tactical Reconnaissance Squadron, 47th Bombardment Wing, flew a night mission for radarscope photography of Soviet cities and military installations. All three aircraft returned safely to a base in West Germany without encountering opposition.

According to the US Defense Department, some forty American aircraft were shot down by Communist Bloc countries between 1950 and 1970. More than 250 aircrew were lost, of whom ninety have never been heard of again. It is not clear how many of these were engaged on spying missions but the RAF did not escape unscathed. On 12 March 1953, a Lincoln bomber from Leconfield in Yorkshire was shot down by MiG fighters after straying into East Germany, and all seven of the crew were killed. It is likely that this loss was due to a navigational error. A sad postscript to this story was that the war medals and documents of one of the crew, Sergeant Peter J. Dunnell,

RB-45 BE-027 of the 19th Tactical Reconnaissance Sqn. (David Whitaker)

RB-45 BE-027. Aircraft was withdrawn from operational use at Sculthorpe in Sept. 1957. (Richard Jermy)

who came from Deopham in Norfolk, were put up for auction by Lockdales auctioneers in September 2011.[14]

By the mid-1950s the Soviet military had greatly improved their anti-aircraft defences, so much so that Nikita Khrushchev, who became Soviet leader after Joseph Stalin died in 1953, could boast to the US Air Force chief General Nathan Twining during a visit in 1956 that 'if something like a Canberra comes into our airspace it will be shot down. All your Canberras are flying coffins'.[15]

The Lockheed U-2 was developed precisely for intelligence gathering (later seen at Sculthorpe). This came to a spectacular climax with the shooting down in 1960 of the CIA (Central Intelligence Agency) U-2 of Gary Powers, which had taken off from Pakistan. His imprisonment in the Soviet Union for spying brought to an end manned overflights behind the Iron Curtain. Powers was released and returned to the United States in February 1962 in exchange for a high-ranking Soviet spy.

In later years, satellite surveillance from space replaced manned aerial reconnaissance, although the details of the RAF overflights only emerged in public view as late as February 1994 in a *Daily Telegraph* article headed: 'The night the RAF "bombed" Russia: British pilots flew spy missions for America'.[16]

NOTES

1. Andrew, Christopher, *The Defence of the Realm: The Authorized History of MI5,* p.390.
2. Ibid. p.420.
3. Ibid. pp.440–1.
4. Ibid. p.341.
5. Lashmar, Paul, 'Shootdowns', *Aeroplane Monthly,* Aug. 1994, pp.8–9.
6. Hall, R. Cargill, *Early Cold War Overflights 1950–56: Symposium Proceedings: An Introduction,* pp.1–2.
7. Lashmar, Paul, *Spy Flights of the Cold War,* p.65.
8. Later Air Marshal Sir Harold Martin KCB, DSO, DFC, AFC.
9. Hall, R. Cargill, *Early Cold War Overflights,* p.4.
10. Crampton, Sqn Ldr John, 'RB-45 Operations', *Air Intelligence Symposium* (Royal Air Force Historical Society, p.122).
11. Ibid. p.122.
12. Lloyd, Alwyn T., *A Cold War Legacy,* p.188.
13. Crampton, Sqn Ldr John, 'RB-45 Operations', p.123.
14. *Eastern Daily Press,* 17 Sept. 2011.
15. *Daily Telegraph,* 7 Feb. 1994: 'The night the RAF "bombed" Russia.'
16. *Daily Telegraph,* 2 Aug. 2010, obit. John Crampton. Also BBC *Timewatch* programme 'Spies in the Sky', Feb. 1994.

9. 47TH BOMBARDMENT WING AND THE FIRST JET BOMBER

'You were either an instrument pilot to begin with, or you became an instrument flier, or you went home in a pine box.'

J.C. Fredriksen, *The B-45 Tornado*

The early 1950s introduced a step-change in American nuclear strategy. While the Korean War was diverting the attentions of the Western powers, there was the danger that the Soviet Union would use its massive military forces to make a move in Western Europe, NATO's vulnerable back door. Accordingly, American policy was now to bring into service a new generation of tactical or battlefield nuclear weapons, along with the means of delivering them: the first all-jet bomber, the North American B-45 Tornado. The outcome was the Mark 5 atomic bomb or 'special weapon' and the programme to modify the B-45 to carry it, code-named Project 'Back Breaker', literally to break the back of any Soviet assault on Europe.

The 49th Air Division was created within the US Air Force's Tactical Air Command (TAC) under the command of Brigadier General John D. Stevenson, the component parts being the reactivated 47th Bombardment Wing, equipped with the B-45 Tornado, and the atomic capable F-84G Thunderjets of the 20th Fighter-Bomber Wing. The establishment of the 49th Air Division Headquarters and the 47th Bomb Wing with its two squadrons, the 84th and 85th, were moved to Sculthorpe on a permanent basis from Langley Air Force Base in Virginia during May and June 1952. The squadrons of the 20th FBW were divided between Wethersfield in Essex and Woodbridge in Suffolk. This amounted to

Insignia of 47th Bomb Wing. (1953 Yearbook)

Insignias of 84th and 85th Bomb Squadrons. (1955 Yearbook)

something like a second 'friendly invasion' some ten years after the first in 1942.

The 47th Bomb Wing was commanded by Colonel David M. Jones who had been a flight commander on General Jimmy Doolittle's famous raid on Tokyo in 1942, the first American air assault on Japan after the attack on Pearl Harbor. Later, he took part in the North African campaign but was shot down and captured, ending up in German prisoner of war camps where he acquired the nickname 'Tokyo' Jones because of his earlier exploits. He took an active part in the tunnelling at Stalag Luft 3, which was eventually to lead to the 'Great Escape' of seventy-six prisoners of war, but by the time of the actual escape the Americans had been moved to another compound – a fact which may have well saved his life, as fifty of the escaped prisoners were subsequently recaptured and executed by the Gestapo.

The Wing was originally formed in January 1941 as a light bomber group and saw action in North Africa and Italy during the Second World War, where it was awarded two Presidential Unit Citations for distinguished service. After a short period of deactivation it was reconstituted in March 1951 with two of its original squadrons, the 84th and 85th.

TRANSIT AND ARRIVAL

The main body of the 47th Wing sailed from Newport News, Virginia, on board the troopship USS *General Hahn* on 21 May 1952, disembarking at Southampton and continuing by train to King's Lynn by the end of the month. The curious logic of military movements was summed up by one airman as: 'The Army flew over, the Navy flew over, the Marines flew over, but the Air Force went by boat.'[1]

The journey was then in the hands of M&GN (The Midland and Great Northern Railway) from South Lynn to Fakenham, via Gayton Road, Grimston Road, Massingham, East Rudham and Raynham Park.

One of the 47th Wing airmen was Donald Hall, a sergeant radar technician with the 84th Bomb Squadron. He sailed to Southampton with the main body of personnel (about 3,000 in all), departing from there on Saturday morning, 31 May 1952, and finding himself at Sculthorpe at about nine o'clock at night. The train travelled through the outskirts of London but beyond that he found the countryside very beautiful but there were some things which seemed strange. In a letter to his sweetheart (and future wife), he described his first impressions of England:

> There are very few cars to be seen and everyone rides a bicycle. Nearly all the houses are made of brick and the yards are very neat and clean, much more so than in the States.

Donald had originally been accepted into the Coast Guard Academy in New London, Connecticut, but at his first medical he was rejected because of a football injury to his front teeth. So with no academy place, not attending college and with the Korean War at its height he was summoned to the draft board, which graded him 1-A fit. Instead of the army, he opted to enlist in the air force on 1 September 1950. After basic training, he was assigned to become an airborne radar technician and was schooled in the latest top-secret system. 'We could not take notebook or paper to class and nothing in writing was ever given to us. We just had to memorise it all.'[2] After training he was assigned to Strategic Air Command as a crewman on the B-36 'Peacemaker' before being posted on flight status to the 47th Bomb Wing at Langley.

The Wing's arrival was also recalled by Donald Aspinall, who was posted to Sculthorpe at the end of May with the 47th Air Police Squadron, the first of three tours of duty he was to serve at Sculthorpe. A first generation American whose mother hailed from Glasgow and his father from Liverpool, Donald was already, at the age of 20, a hardened war veteran from Korea. He had enlisted when he was 15 in the Army Air Corps and found himself at gunnery school for B-29 bombers. He became a waist gunner on the aircraft port side and in 1950 was transferred to Yokota in Japan for missions over North Korea. On Wednesday 13 March 1951, his aircraft was shot down over 'Mig Alley' – the Chosin River area – and he bailed out at 18,000ft. All twelve of the crew were captured:

> ... and for nine days were headed in the wrong direction. We outnumbered our Chinese captors (there were four of them) and managed to escape and make it back to our lines. Fourteen days later we were back over the same area in North Korea, armed and bombed the hell out of it.

In January 1952, Donald Aspinall was transferred to Langley Air Force Base to join the 47th Wing for training prior to the move to England.[3]

The aerial units began to depart from Langley on 6 June, the first eight B-45s flying via Goose Bay, Labrador and Iceland, after intensive training in ditching, air-sea rescue procedures and water-survival techniques. By 12 June, both squadrons, the 84th and 85th, had safely reassembled at Sculthorpe, making this 'a significant historical event being the first ever, mass Atlantic flyover by large, jet-powered aircraft'.[4]

47th Air Police Sqn. insignia. (Donald Aspinall)

FIRST IMPRESSIONS AND SETTLING IN

Tragedy struck the first night of the 47th's arrival when an airman (a member of ground crew) was killed by a lightning strike at the base, as recalled by Verrall Grimes, who worked as a civilian in the NCO Club. This might well have been the event experienced by Donald Aspinall at about the same time: he and two others were walking across a baseball field to go to the Exchange when they were hit by lightning. 'There was myself, Al Anona and Jim Tesario. Al died on the spot and Jim and I were kept in the hospital overnight for observation. We both had headaches and that was all – Thank God!'[5]

First impressions of Sculthorpe for the Americans were bleak. For one airman 'its only significant claim to fame was for being obliterated by the Black Plague during the Middle Ages'.[6] In spite of the building and development work of recent years during the frequent TDYs of the bomber units, there was still a dearth of comfort and amenities. The TDYs seem to have been part of the problem as the intervals between deployments had led to neglect, disrepair and even vandalism. Windows had been left broken, doors hanging off their hinges and there had been little incentive for the 'TDYers' to tidy up before departure. GI blankets had proved their worth in curtaining the gaps in doors and windows.[7]

Corrugated Quonset huts, of US design based on the British Nissen huts, were supplemented by temporary wooden huts. The Quonset huts could sleep ten men, and were put to other uses, like the commissary and Base Exchange buildings.

As a sergeant, Donald Hall was probably luckier than many single men in that he lived in one of the recently completed 'Z' blocks divided into single rooms – 'only that there are two of us in each room. Typical of the Air Force', as he wrote to his sweetheart.

The spartan conditions could only deteriorate as winter approached, with the cold and damp to contend with. One officer recalled his accommodation: 'It wasn't a Quonset hut, but a cinder block-type structure with no installed heat. I used to wear fur-lined boots!'[8]

There was some relief with coal-burning stoves and 'Aladdin' heaters, but when the opportunity arose there was an escape to the social amenities of the NCO and Officers' Messes of nearby RAF stations. In Sculthorpe the Officers' Club, or Mess, and it certainly was – had a place where they could eat and drink, but it was the private consensus that the small, cold and limited facilities could only drive you to drink.'[9]

As Sergeant Donald Hall began to settle in, he wrote home that:

the English money is fairly easy to learn but the people sure have a funny way of talking, but I am getting on to it already. The base is miles from nowhere and there is only one bus leaving the base each day, so I guess I won't be wandering around except to play golf and go to London once a month or so. It costs £1.00, one pound equals $2.80, for a round-trip train ticket to London from here, which is very cheap and it takes about six hours.'[10] [Nothing much seems to have changed, except for the price.]

The state of the roads were also a shock for the new arrivals and 'the overall scene was more of a ghost-station than an actual operating station of the USAF'.[11]

It was by no means all doom and gloom. The fire department was rated among the best. Bowling alleys had to be painted on the floor of the service club. Beer cans served as the first pins until the authentic looking pins and small wooden balls arrived in an early shipment from the States. Donald Hall had plenty of scope for playing golf. He came from a family of professional golfers and wasted no time in applying to join the Brancaster Golf Club, whose members welcomed the young American to their ranks.

Sgt Donald Hall's Riley Kestrel outside Z blocks, winter 1953. To the left is the NCO Club complex. (Donald Hall)

The same Z block site
in 2013. (Author)

"*It doesn't rain over here all the time, but . . .*"

Cartoon from *1957 in
England.*

AIRCRAFT AND THE MISSION

Early visitors to the 47th Bomb Wing included Lieutenant General Lauris Norstad, Commanding General of Allied Air Forces, Europe, and Mr T.K. Finletter, US Air Force Secretary, who did a tour of inspection in the middle of June. Apart from the B-45s of the 84th and 85th Bomb Squadrons there were also present some of the transport components of the 49th Air Division including the 60th Troop Carrier Wing (TCW) equipped with the C-119 Fairchild Packet, sometimes referred to as 'Flying Boxcars', and the L20 (De Havilland Beaver), a utility transport aircraft. In addition, a common sight at Sculthorpe were the C-47s (DC-3) transport aircraft – Dakotas or 'Goony Birds' in USAF parlance – and on occasions the Second World War vintage B-26 as target tugs, a type formerly part of the wing's equipment as a light bomber. A Lockheed T-33A two-seat advanced jet trainer met the requirement for continuous training.

But the B-45 Tornados were the 'fist' of the 49th Air Division. A total of about forty-five aircraft made up the complement. The B-45 had four General Electric J47-GE-15 jet engines, two on each wing. They were in pods next to each other and enclosed as one. Sometimes jet pods were also used for take-off if additional weight was being carried. The aircraft spanned nearly 90ft, had a maximum speed of 570mph (about 0.76 Mach) and was said to be capable of remaining airborne for about 4½ hours. As late as March 1955 no precise details of the aircraft's range had been published, according to *Flight* magazine,[12] but it was estimated to be in the region of 500–700 miles. It was claimed that the B-45 could not be air-refuelled, in contrast to the air-refuelling capacity of the RB-45C during the 'secret flights' of April 1952 and April 1954 (see Chapter Eight), but this was information that did not

B-45s 7078 and 7066 of 85th Bomb Sqn. These aircraft were in operational use at Sculthorpe from 1952 until withdrawal from service in 1958. (M. J. F. Bowyer)

C-47 of 49th Air Division with car, summer 1954. (M. J. F. Bowyer)

Fairchild Packet C-119C Flying Boxcar of 49th Air Division, with tower in background. (M. J. F. Bowyer)

come to light until much later. However, it was admitted that the range would be considerably extended by the two under-nacelle 500-gallon external tanks and the extra fuel tank mounted in the bomb bay. With a crew of four – two pilots in tandem under the canopy, a navigator/bombardier down in the nose and a tail gunner – the aircraft had a maximum operational ceiling of just over 46,000ft. The bomb bay was designed to accommodate a bomb load of up to 22,000lbs, conventional or atomic. The average length of missions was expected to be around 3¼ hours, mainly single aircraft raids within the European theatre, in high-level support of the ground forces and well within the range of European Russia.

No time was lost in becoming operational. There were several night interdiction exercises aimed at targets in Western Europe. In the event of war, the interdiction operation would have the function of delaying, disrupting or destroying enemy forces before they reached the battlefield. There was no doubt about the ultimate purpose of the 47th, the first American unit assigned to NATO forces that was capable of delivering atomic bombs. The B-45 was capable of carrying so-called 'special weapons' of the appropriate weight and size to simulate the Mark 5 atomic weapon. In Norfolk, there were frequent exercises in the use of such dummy bombs but care was taken to discharge the weapons discreetly out to sea and not by mistake in a local farmer's field.[13] For a time the range at Luce Bay in Galloway was used for practice bombing from a height of about 36,000ft.

Even today, the activities of the 47th Wing are shrouded in secrecy. There is anecdotal evidence that reconnaissance missions were flown over or close to Soviet territory on occasions. As part of combat readiness, targets had been assigned in the event of war, but given the limited range of the B-45 and the heavy air defences to overcome, it was generally accepted that any bombing operations would be one-way tickets for the crews, with little chance of a successful return to the home base. In any case, the home base would be targeted by Soviet bombers while the B-45s were en route to their first strike.

Robert Boudreau was a weather forecaster with the 47th Wing and he still marvels at the fact that he was only 21 years of age when he was preparing weather forecasts for the possible atomic bombing of Russia. 'We were in a constant state of readiness to attack.'[14]

Donald Aspinall of the 47th Air Police Squadron recalled that he was among those selected for duty in 'The Shooting Box', South Creake, which was an off base command and communications centre with its own sleeping quarters and mess hall. During practice alerts Donald would often be sent there and would stand behind a huge lined board with headset and microphone in contact with pilots during flights (see also Chapter Eleven).[15]

B-45 7027 of 85th Bomb Sqn, tower in background. Aircraft in operational use at Sculthorpe from 1952 until withdrawn from service in 1958. (M. J. F. Bowyer)

One hazard closer to home was the Norfolk weather, so different from the milder conditions of the home base in Virginia. Fog, rain and poor visibility meant increasing reliance on GCA (ground control approach radar), which involved the air traffic controllers using radar to guide an aircraft to a safe landing – a technique extensively used during the Berlin Airlift. This became even more vital with the onset of autumn and winter. One pilot observed that 'you were either an instrument pilot to begin with, or you became an instrument flier, or you went home in a pine box'.[16]

An air rescue unit had been in place at Sculthorpe since around August 1951. The 9th Air Rescue Squadron had arrived from Manston with four SB-29s and remained until 1953. Other detachments of the squadron, which included Grumman SA-16A Albatross amphibians, served at Burtonwood and Bentwaters. The personnel included four flight crews and maintenance staff, one of the latter being Sergeant Bill Tollefson, part of the team which carried out regular inspections and maintenance of each aircraft after every 200 hours' flying time. His specific job was to check No. 2 engine on each aircraft. He recalled that the aircraft carried a lifeboat as well as oxygen supplies and provisions, along with an inflatable cover for the lifeboat to protect it from high seas.

Bill had joined the air force in 1949 from high school near Lake Superior in Michigan, at a time when there were few jobs available. His friends at high school thought he was mad to join the air force but soon changed their tune when the Korean War broke out and they realised that the air force was a better option than being drafted into the infantry! During his training in airplane maintenance on the

67th Air Rescue Sqn at Sculthorpe with unidentified airman. Note motto 'That Others May Live'. (Flt Sgt Mark Service and J. Maiden)

B-29, at least half of his fellow classmates were posted to Okinawa for possible service in the Korean War. Bill found himself in Britain with the 9th Air Rescue Squadron, first at Manston and then from August 1951 at Sculthorpe where he remained until March 1953. He met his future wife in Sculthorpe (see Chapter Twelve).

He recalled a typical mission at the time being the escorting of fighters over the Atlantic in case one of them was forced to ditch. On another occasion, an aircraft was called out to drop oxygen supplies to a freighter in the mid-Atlantic for a sick crewman.

The 67th Air Rescue Squadron was formed at Sculthorpe on 14 November 1952, equipped with a variety of aircraft, which included the SA-16A Albatross and the SB-29 'Super Dumbo'. The latter was a Boeing B-29 bomber converted for an air-sea rescue role, adapted for long-range missions and featuring an A3 air-droppable lifeboat. The unit also comprised a C-82A Packet support aircraft, later replaced by a C-47. The squadron moved to Prestwick on 4 November 1953. Today the squadron is designated the 67th Special Operations Squadron and is based at RAF Mildenhall.[17] The squadron celebrated its sixtieth anniversary during the weekend of 10–11 November 2012 (see Chapter Ten).

A3 Lifeboat. (Flt Sgt Mark Service)

A3 Lifeboat parachuted during exercise. (Flt Sgt Mark Service)

Boeing SB-29 dropping Lifeboat. (Flt Sgt Mark Service)

Boeing SB-29 with Lifeboat. (Flt Sgt Mark Service)

Boeing SB-29 dropping Lifeboat. (Flt Sgt Mark Service)

NOTES

1. Fredriksen, J.C., *The B-45 Tornado,* pp.117–18.
2. Hall, Donald, email to author, 17 June 2012.
3. Aspinall, Donald, emails to author, 24 Aug. and 5 Sept. 2011.
4. Fredriksen, p.118.
5. Aspinall, Donald, email, 26 Aug. 2011.
6. Fredriksen, p.118.
7. *1957 in England:* A Souvenir of the 47th BW, USAF, 1957.
8. Fredriksen, pp.118–19.
9. *1957 in England.*
10. Hall, Donald, email, 19 June 2012.
11. *1957 in England.*
12. Flightglobal Archive, 25 March 1955.
13. Fredriksen, p.120.
14. Boudreau, Robert, email to author, 20 March 2009.
15. Aspinall, Donald, email, Dec. 2012.
16. Fredriksen, p.121.
17. Service, Flt Sgt Mark, Squadron Historian, 67th Special Operations Sqn.

10. 1953 FLOODS — TRAGEDY AND HEROISM

'Norfolk Gale Disaster … Seas' wild rush into Towns and Villages.'

(*Eastern Daily Press*, Monday 2 February 1953)

It was the night of Saturday 31 January 1953 and as many people living along the coast settled down for a relaxing evening listening to the radio or planned to meet up with friends and family, little did they know that many of them were about to face the worst evening of their lives. The weather took a vicious turn during the late evening when a combination of hurricane-force winds and an abnormally high tide lashed the east coast of Britain and the coasts of Belgium and the Netherlands, setting in motion the worst floods in recorded history.

More than 300 people from Scotland to Kent lost their lives and around 24,000 homes were lost or destroyed. In Norfolk, the toll was 100 lives lost and thousands of families made homeless as their houses were swept away. In King's Lynn fifteen people were drowned, as were twenty-five at Snettisham, nine at Heacham and thirty-one at Hunstanton's South Beach Road, losses which included sixteen Americans who were from families associated with the base at Sculthorpe. Many of the American victims had been living in wooden prefabricated houses in low-lying communities along the coast from Snettisham and Heacham to Hunstanton. These 'austerity' homes, built rapidly to ease the post-war housing shortages, were easy prey to the waves, which rose to 16ft in height, and gales which topped 100mph.

All the available emergency services sprang into action, not least among them the personnel at Sculthorpe, many of whom risked their own lives in the rescue operation. There was much heroism that night among the police, rescue services and ordinary members of the public, without whom many more lives would have been lost. Notable among the American airmen was 22-year-old Airman Second Class Reis L. Leming of the 67th Air Rescue Squadron who, although a non-swimmer, braved the tides three times to tow a small six-man rubber raft in a rescue attempt. Clad in an anti-exposure suit, which soon became snagged and holed by underwater

Reis Leming before completing training and joining 67th Air Rescue Sqn. (Leming family)

obstacles, he was often neck-deep in water and in total darkness. After his third trip, he was forced to abandon the effort due to near collapse with hypothermia and exhaustion but had successfully rescued twenty-seven people. As he recalled later: 'It was cold, bitterly cold. And there came a time when I realised that I, too, was probably not going to survive.'[1]

Verrall Grimes, who worked in the NCO Club, knew Reis well: 'He was very tall and used to come into the Club where I worked. He would buy me things I needed from the PX (the supermarket on the base) [...] in the floods they dropped dinghies from the B-29s and Reis waded into water up to his waist.'

Army cooks of the 39th Anti-Aircraft Artillery (AAA) Battalion from Sculthorpe were later commended for serving 1,400 meals on the morning of the tragedy. There was water everywhere but no fresh water to drink as salt water had inundated the supply, so that salt water was coming out of the taps. Long before the days of bottled water, personnel from Sculthorpe came to the rescue again with tankers of fresh water. One resident recalled 'standing in a queue of people, all with our buckets'.[2] Roland Axman remembered the scene in Hunstanton:

> The Sunday after the floods you would have thought somebody had been around Hunstanton with a massive drill – slabs of concrete everywhere – ten foot square lifted up and all the caravans wrecked. I had to take a vanload of bread (he worked for Waggs the Bakers in Docking) to the emergency centre in King's Lynn and I talked to one chap whose house had been flooded out in south Lynn.[3]

Staff Sergeant Jewel M. 'Nip' Smart belonged to the 47th Medical Group at Sculthorpe and was involved in the rescue and recovery of the Americans lost in the Hunstanton tidal wave that day. He was later to have the sombre task of escorting six bodies of the victims to the RAF station at Burtonwood for return to the United States.

Day after the floods in Hunstanton – the house on the right was a two-storey house. The other house was washed up against it. (Jewel M. 'Nip' Smart)

Floods aftermath in Hunstanton. (Jewel M. 'Nip' Smart)

Reis Leming's bravery was recognised by the awards of the Soldier's Medal of the United States and the George Medal of the United Kingdom, the first given to a foreigner during peacetime, presented by the Home Secretary, Sir David Maxwell Fyfe. Later, several other Americans were granted awards for their bravery that night: Staff Sergeant Freeman A. Kilpatrick, also received the George Medal; The Queen's Commendation for Brave Conduct went to Airman First Class Jimmy Brown and Technical Sergeant John G. Germaine; the British Empire Medal was awarded to Airman First Class Jake J. Smith, and Major Julian E. Perkinson was made an honorary member of the Order of the British Empire, Military Division.

The tragedy that day did much to cement Anglo-American relations and contributed much to the generally good community relations that have endured over the years. A member of the Hunstanton Town Council, Frank Sawbridge, contributed a slate plaque to commemorate those who lost their lives at Hunstanton, which was dedicated in August 1953. In May of the following year, the Lord Lieutenant of Norfolk, Sir Edmund Bacon, presented a silver cock pheasant to the base commander at Sculthorpe, Colonel David M. Jones, a gift to which the people of Norfolk had contributed, in recognition of the help the Americans had given during the floods.[4] When the 47th Bomb Wing was deactivated in June 1962, the silver pheasant was given to the governors of the Memorial Trust of the 2nd Air Division Association USAAF for display in the 2nd Air Division Memorial Library. Sadly, the gift was destroyed in the fire that burned down the library and memorial room on 1 August 1994. However, an almost identical replacement was found which is now on display in the 2nd Air Division Library at the Forum in Norwich.

The bravery of Reis that terrible day was never forgotten by the people of Hunstanton and he became a local hero. When he married his childhood sweetheart, Mary Joan Ramsey, in June 1953, the ceremony took place at the Roman Catholic Church in Hunstanton and the town insisted on organising the event. Wedding presents included a set of Doulton china from the townspeople, and local ladies pooled their rations to make a wedding cake.

S/Sgt Freeman A. Kilpatrick receiving his George Medal from Sir Maxwell Fyfe. (1953 Pictorial)

The Silver Pheasant replica (2nd Air Division Memorial Library, Norwich). (Author)

Ceremony at Hunstanton, 10 November 2012, with 'Reis Leming' sign. In foreground is Hunstanton Memorial to the Flood Victims. (Author)

67th Special Operations Sqn USAF parade at Hunstanton for 60th Anniversary Commemoration of floods, 31 Jan. 2013. Lt Col Shelley Rodriguez on right. In centre Flt Sgt Mark
Service, 67th Sqn historian. (Author)

Long after he left Sculthorpe he made several return trips to the town, including
on the occasion of the fortieth anniversary memorial service in 1993. During this
visit he was invited to meet the Queen and Queen Mother at Sandringham.

On the fiftieth anniversary of the floods in 2003, Reis and his wife made another
emotional return to Hunstanton. The memories were still undimmed: 'For 50 years
I have woken up some nights and wondered: Was it all a mirage? Did I really save all
those people? Did they really survive?' He later summed up his experiences as 'being
in the wrong place at the right time'.

Reis Leming was due to return to Hunstanton on Saturday 10 November 2012
as part of the celebrations for the sixtieth anniversary of the 67th Special Operations
Squadron (formerly the 67th Air Rescue Squadron), now based at Mildenhall. Sadly,
he died one day short of his 82nd birthday on 5 November, only days before the
event, but was remembered during the squadron's anniversary parade held in the
town. There was a brief ceremony at the memorial to the flood victims and a new
road sign named 'Reis Leming Way' in his honour was unveiled by the squadron
commander, Lieutenant Colonel Shelley Rodriguez.[5]

The sixtieth anniversary commemoration of the 1953 floods was held at
Hunstanton on Thursday 31 January 2013, at which Reis' widow, Kathy, daughter,
Debra, and son, Michael, were present. The 67th Squadron personnel, with their

commander, Lieutenant Colonel Rodriguez, once again paraded in the town. A brief ceremony was held at the floods memorial, followed by a service at the Parish Church of St Edmund, Hunstanton.

NOTES

1. BBC News website.
2. *Eastern Daily Press,* letters, Ernest Hoyos, 18 Feb. 2013.
3. Roland Axman, interview with author, 6 May 2012.
4. *1957 in England.*
5. Information from Flt Sgt Mark Service, Squadron Historian, 67th Special Operations Sqn.

11. SCULTHORPE'S HEYDAY (1953–56)

'No one stood between us and those pesky Russians.'

The early to mid-1950s saw the build-up of the US Third Air Force tactical bomber force in Britain centred on the 49th Air Division, with headquarters at Sculthorpe where the B-45 Tornados of the 47th Bomb Wing were based. The other components of the division were the F-84G Thunderjets of the 20th Fighter-Bomber Wing at Woodbridge and Wethersfield and, from the spring of 1954, F-84G Thunderjets of the 81st Fighter-Bomber Wing at Bentwaters.

The emphasis was now on tactical (i.e. medium-range battlefield) rather than strategic nuclear weaponry, which provided much more flexibility to commanders should a war break out in Europe. Technological advances had also produced bombs of a more manageable size since 1950, with a relatively small device now available, weighing around 2,000lbs (one-fifth of the weight of the Hiroshima bomb), capable of being carried by the F-84G Thunderjets. US atomic policy was now, in President Eisenhower's words, 'not to cause more destruction – but to find out ways and means in which you can limit it [...] make it more of a military weapon and less one of just mass destruction'.[1]

Sculthorpe was at the height of its importance in the period 1952 to 1956, when the 49th Air Division was head-quartered there with the 47th Bomb

1953 Air Pictorial. (Flt Sgt Mark Service)

DHC L-20A Beaver of the 47th Operations Sqn. (M. J. F. Bowyer)

Wing as the resident unit. Other units came and went, but at its height the base hosted 10,000 personnel and their dependants and anything up to 100 aircraft. The B-45 Tornados of the 47th Bomb Wing represented the main offensive 'punch', with forty to fifty aircraft operational at any one time. Other types present included the venerable C-47 Skytrain, the C-119 Flying Boxcar, L20 Beaver, and Lockheed T-33 for transport and communications. The SA-16 Albatross and SB-29s of the 67th Air Rescue Squadron provided the vital search and rescue role. The base must have been an airplane spotter's paradise.

A new arrival from Bentwaters was the 7554th Tow Target Flight (TTF) on 16 December 1952 with its TB-26 Invaders to tow targets at Stiffkey Camp near Weybourne on the Norfolk coast, providing target practice for the anti-aircraft gunners of the US Army. To assist with liaison duties the Tow Target Flight also used a few L-5 Sentinels. In June 1954, the unit changed its designation to become a detachment of the 5th Target Tow Squadron, the parent unit being based at Fürstenfeldbruck, West Germany. Piston-engined pilotless drones were also flown at Weybourne Camp for the anti-aircraft gunners operated by the 50th Radio Controlled Airplane Target Detachment.

Other US Army units present during the 1950s included the 172nd Chemical Smoke Company and the 39th Antiaircraft Artillery (AAA) Battalion.

In June 1953, a mock attack on the airfield was mounted by British Army Territorial Army (TA) units, no doubt to flex their muscles while at annual summer camp. The attacking force included the 13th (Lancashire) Battalion of the Parachute Regiment (TA) and various other engineer, medical and workshop units. Parachutists were dropped by the C-119 Fairchild Packets (Flying Boxcars) and there was a midnight diversionary raid on the airfield perimeter by about twenty men, which was reported to have breached the perimeter fencing in several places.

TB-26B Invader of the 7554th Target Towing Flight, later det. of 5th Target Towing Sqn. (M. J. F. Bowyer)

Stinson L-5 Sentinel, also used by Target Towing Flight. (M. J. F. Bowyer)

Insignia of the 39th AAA Battalion. (1953 Pictorial)

The 67th Air Rescue Squadron was present throughout much of 1953. Equipment on the unit's strength in August included four SB-29 'Super Dumbo' aircraft (serials 42-63750, 44-86303, 44-86308 and 44-86355). Support was provided by the C-82A Packet (serial 48-0568), which later replaced by a C-47. Two SB-29s from the squadron were among aircraft that went to assist in the rescue of a crew from a Convair B-36 which crashed in the Atlantic on 5 August on its way from California to Lakenheath. Each dropped a lifeboat but the sea was too rough to enable an SA-16 flying boat to touch down. In the end it was left to a sea search, and only four survivors from the total of twenty-three crew and passengers were picked up.

Shortly after arrival in Prestwick, an SB-29 (serial 44-86308) was itself involved in a full-scale emergency when its No. 3 engine failed during a night training flight off the coast of Norway. A few minutes out of Prestwick the propeller overspeeded and sheared off, causing severe damage to the aircraft and the failure of No. 4 engine. The landing gear failed to extend fully, and the pilot, Captain Ridenour, had no choice but to make a wheels-up crash landing. All ten crew members survived but the aircraft was written-off.[2]

SCULTHORPE'S PUNCH

The North American B-45 Tornado represented the main offensive equipment of the US Air Force at Sculthorpe. In the words of one veteran: 'No one stood between us and those pesky Russians'. In spite of a worrying series of malfunctions and accidents, 1953 proved to be a busy year for the 47th Wing. There was frequent fighter interception training with Meteors from West Raynham, and Royal Navy Hawker Sea Hawks which tested the agility of the B-45s to avoid interception. In the majority of cases the B-45 proved its worth. There were exercises throughout Europe and across the Atlantic to test the efficiency and speed of deployments in diverse environments. Nearer to home, there was a shortage of suitable practice bombing ranges but use was made of sites like Luce Bay in Galloway, Scotland. At the end of the year, the 422nd Bombardment

Sculthorpe's 'Punch' – the B-45s of the 47th Bomb Wing. (Jewel M. 'Nip' Smart)

Squadron joined the 47th Wing, to be activated as the 86th Bomb Squadron in March 1954, composed of crews from the 84th and 85th Squadrons.

1954 – THE 'LID' FINALLY COMES OFF

Joseph Stalin had died in March 1953, giving way to a struggle for power in the USSR which would lead to a new leader of the Soviet Union emerging by the end of 1954, Nikita Khrushchev. Any hope that this might lead to a lessening in international tension was soon dispelled by his hostile rhetoric and the build-up of Soviet nuclear capability. The Soviets were very close behind the United States in building a hydrogen bomb, as well as the means of delivering such weapons by a new generation of long-range strategic bombers. The purpose of the 'secret flights' (see Chapter Eight) was to monitor how far the Soviet Union had progressed in these developments. Another factor to take into account was the threat of communist expansion in Southeast Asia and the Third World, in which Russia and China appeared to be acting in concert.

In September 1953 there was a clarification of previous agreements about the use of American bases in Britain in the event of war. Prime Minister Winston Churchill repeated in the House of Commons that it would be a matter of a 'joint decision' between the UK and US governments for any US offensive action from the bases to be taken in the event of an emergency. The general consensus was that the American bases in the UK were here to stay. At the same time, a detailed agreement as to the breakdown of costs of the bases shared between the American and British governments was released.

By the start of 1954, Britain had a credible nuclear deterrent in the 'Blue Danube' atomic bomb, while the Americans were building up a nuclear stockpile in Britain. Tactical nuclear weapons were under secure storage at Sculthorpe by the middle of the year.[3] The difference now was that some of these facts were beginning to come into the open in a way that had never happened previously.

On 22 January 1954, the *New York Times* produced an article outlining the atomic training undertaken by the 47th Wing before arrival in England and some of the clandestine missions flown by the B-45s in the direction of Russia's southern borders. These revelations enabled the commanding general of the 49th Air Division, Brigadier General Stevenson, to request that the highly classified status of the division be relaxed to a more realistic level in keeping with what was already known in the public domain.[4]

Much could be done to cement already good relationships with the local community. Following on from Battle of Britain anniversary celebrations, the first open day at Sculthorpe was held on 29 May 1954. It was by all accounts sparsely attended, probably more due to transport difficulties than to lack of interest.

But the cat was well and truly out of the bag with a series of articles penned by Anthony Brown in the *Daily Mail* during December 1954, who claimed to be the first British reporter to tour the 'American atom-bomb base in England'. Headlined 'Mail Man Tours Atom Base', the article described a visit to Sculthorpe conducted by Colonel John D. Glover, deputy commander of the base, which he claimed to be 'the biggest and most vital jet bombardment base in western Europe'.

Anthony Brown recalled being driven within ten yards of a 'single tin shed' where the weapons 'of massive retaliation' were stored in a concrete chamber deep underground, guarded by airmen carrying carbines. Not far away stood 'the planes which could be within two hours on their way to strike, loaded with nuclear weapons – the 400mph Tornado bombers'.

Later in his account he described the lives of the 3,500 airmen on the base, fed with steaks from Ireland and living in steam-heated quarters.[5] 'Their cigarettes come from America, their whisky from Scotland, their wives' perfume from Paris. Their chocolate is English, their sweaters are of cashmere.' There was no downplaying the role of the base: 'I went to the operations centre. Here the edict is: "Be ready for massive retaliation".' There was no mistaking the tight security around the base and when asked about the nature of the nuclear weapons, there was a 'No Comment' from the commander.

On a lighter note there was a mention of the local policeman, PC Bert Shurety, who had given help 'worth a million dollars … everyone up here on the base loves the guy'. A meeting was arranged with one of the heroes of the flood rescue effort of 1952–53, Technical Sergeant F.A. Kilpatrick GM. His only comment to the reporter was: 'Do I know why I am here? Yes I know. But I get up. I go to work. I come home, eat supper, and go to bed.'

A F84 Thunderstreak pilot, Captain Milton S. Jones, aged 32, summed up his attitude: 'It's an awful responsibility. But there's no point in feeling awed. It is necessary in the defence of our countries.'

The article closed with a mention of the $4,000 collected from the base personnel for children's parties and for presents for the elderly and orphans.[6]

In an article of the previous day, also by Anthony Brown, headed 'Atom Bomb Village Kept its Secret', the opinions of some local villagers 'who can see the atom bomb dump that protects Europe' were commented on. Did they realise that one of the bombs could destroy more buildings and people than all the last war air-fleets in Britain? The answer was 'Yes', but also resignation and acceptance of why the base was there. The memories of the American presence in East Anglia during the last war were still fresh. There was little discussion about the base and more concern about the land and the thought that the Air Ministry might take more of it away. A farmer called Mr Williamson had a barley crop right up to the wire around the bomb dump: 'I never talk. They never talk … but I am glad they are there.' The same sentiment was repeated by the landlord of the local pub, the Horse and Groom: 'I can't remember anyone saying more than a few words about the base.'

'The lid finally comes off' - *Daily Mail* 13 Dec. and 14 Dec. 1954. (*Daily Mail*/Associated Newspapers Ltd)

Colonel David Jones, base commander, summed up his attitude to Sculthorpe:

There is only one place other than Texas – Norfolk. The people are kind and courteous. We go pheasant shooting or wild fowling up in the Wash. My NCOs have a darts team. The local people and the police come to supper parties. We go to your homes. Yes sir, I can say that Sculthorpe is a fine place to be.[7]

THE REACTION

The Soviet Union was quick to react to these revelations. The *Daily Mail* ran an article on 18 December 1954 with the headline: 'That Sculthorpe Base: Now Russians Attack Us'. An official note had been delivered by the Russian Chargé d'Affaires in London to Sir Ivone Kirkpatrick, Permanent Under-Secretary at the Foreign Office, complaining about the recent reports about Sculthorpe and the US atomic capability, accusing Britain of impairing the spirit of her 1942 friendship treaty with Russia. Even in Britain there was some disquiet. George Wigg, Labour MP for Dudley, asked the attorney general in a parliamentary question whether the *Daily Mail* should be prosecuted under the Official Secrets Act for revealing particulars of places where atomic weapons were stored.

There was no doubt that Sculthorpe now stood at the heart of NATO's defence policy as a major nuclear base. This was all happening at the time of high-level talks within NATO to cement the alliance and to affirm that atomic weapons would be used the moment war broke out in Europe. Under the *Daily Mail* heading 'Britain Plunges for A-Weapons – Only deterrent which may make the Soviets hesitate', the NATO General Council was reported to have agreed that 'if Russia made an all-out atomic attack, General Gruenther [NATO Supreme Commander] could immediately order the atomic bombers at Sculthorpe, Norfolk, and other tactical atomic weapons under him into action *without awaiting Government authority*'.[8] (author's italics).

UNIT AND PERSONNEL MOVEMENTS IN 1954 AND 1955

The third bomb squadron of the 47th Wing, the 86th, was activated by March 1954 and was due to spend eighteen months at Sculthorpe before transferring to Alconbury on 15 September of the following year, a move designed to assist in the sensible policy of dispersing units where possible. During 1955, Alconbury had been designated a satellite station of Sculthorpe, until it achieved independent status at the end of the year.

The clandestine activities of the base had been further strengthened in May 1954 by the arrival from Shaw Air Force Base, South Carolina, of the 19th Tactical Reconnaissance Squadron (Night Photographic) of the 66th Tactical Reconnaissance

Crest of 86th Bomb Sqn. (1955 Yearbook)

Wing (TRW) with its RB-45Cs, now to join the 47th Bomb Wing. The unit's task was photographic reconnaissance along the fringes of Eastern Europe (and into the Soviet Union – see Chapter Eight). The squadron commander Major John B. Anderson was a seasoned veteran, having flown Lockheed P-38 Lightnings in the Second World War and Douglas RB-26 Invaders over Korea.

Among the new arrivals at Sculthorpe in early May 1955 was 20-year-old Airman Third Class Wolfgang W.E. Samuel (later Colonel USAF). He was German by birth and had only become an American citizen after he had enlisted in the Air Force from his home town in Colorado. He had already packed more adventures into his early life than most people manage in a lifetime. In 1945, he and his mother had escaped to western Germany just ahead of the sound of the Russian guns, but it was during the Berlin Airlift that he became inspired by the massive American and Allied air bridge to supply the citizens of Berlin, and he determined one day to become an American flyer. In 1951, Wolfgang and his mother managed to sail to America where new opportunities beckoned. The 16-year-old refugee who at first could barely understand a word of English set about working his way through high school and college until at least part of his ambition had been fulfilled in joining the United States Air Force, even as one of the lowest-ranking airman.

At the end of April 1955 he had found himself on the troop transport USS *General Simon B. Buckner* sailing from New York to Southampton. On arrival, he was to be assigned to the 28th Weather Squadron, which provided detachments to American airfields throughout the United Kingdom to gather local weather information and forecasting for the flying units.

From Southampton, transport was laid on for Bushy Park, near London, where Wolfgang was interviewed by Lieutenant Colonel Arnold Hull, commander of Detachment 2, 28th Weather Squadron at Sculthorpe.

Crest of 19th Tactical Reconnaissance Sqn. (1955 Yearbook)

RB-45C 8043 of 19th Tactical Reconnaissance Sqn 1954. Aircraft at Sculthorpe from 1954 until withdrawn from operations in 1957. (M. J. F. Bowyer)

RB-45C 8034 of 19th Tactical Reconnaissance Sqn with T-33 c. 1955. Aircraft at Sculthorpe until withdrawn from operations in 1957. (David Whitaker)

Control Tower in 2011. (Author)

Control Tower in 2013. (Author)

RB-45C 8019 of 19th Tactical Reconnaissance Sqn. Aircraft was at Sculthorpe from 1954 to Aug. 1957 when it was struck off charge. (Mike Hooks)

The colonel was sufficiently impressed to take him on as his administrative clerk and the next day Wolfgang was on his way by train to King's Lynn. He was struck by the similarities between the poor and largely agricultural Norfolk countryside and his native Lüneburg Heath area of Germany. He was warned to expect plenty of rain! Arriving at King's Lynn railway station, he was soon on his way by pickup truck to Sculthorpe, the home of the 47th Bombardment Wing (Medium). It must have been slightly disconcerting for the young airman to be regaled most of the way by the English driver, describing how the German bombers used to cross the Wash during the war, flying so low that the faces of the crew could be seen. 'Other than saying hello and goodbye, I don't believe I added anything to the conversation. I was soon to discover that the Second World War was a topic that would come up continuously when I was with my English friends.'[9]

When processing had been completed, Wolfgang was allocated to a small room in the airmen's barracks (presumably the Z blocks) which he shared with another airman, and as a latecomer he had to be content with the top bunk bed. The 28th Weather Squadron detachment operated from an off-base site called 'The Shooting Box', in South Creake village. This former hunting lodge had been a remote communications and command centre for Sculthorpe since 1944 and was fully self-supporting, with its own cooks and other facilities. In Wolfgang's opinion, 'the little villages of South and North Creek [sic] were much more pleasant environments than the bland functional facilities at Sculthorpe'.[10] The detachment numbered twenty-four men and eleven officers and Wolfgang quickly settled in to his administrative duties.

Armed Forces Day on 21 May 1955 saw around 5,000 Norfolk people descending on the base to view a great variety of American and British aircraft at close quarters. During June, there was a change at the top as Colonel David M. Jones, the famous 'Tokyo Raider' (one of the participants in the first air assault on Japan in 1942 led by General Doolittle), relinquished command of the 47th Bomb Wing after three years in the post. He had guided the unit from its arrival in England to a high state of operational readiness. One of his most cherished ambitions had been to see the opening of a club for airmen of less than NCO rank, believed to be the first of its type in England. Deputy commander Colonel John G. Glover took over the reins for the few months before the new commander arrived in September, Colonel (now promoted to Brigadier General) Joseph R. Holzapple.

General Holzapple was no stranger to Norfolk, having been operations officer at Attlebridge during the war, before distinguished service in North Africa, Italy, France and later the Pacific.

The annual air defence exercise 'Foxpaw' was held at the end of September and start of October, involving 946 fighters of RAF Fighter Command opposing forces of USAF bombers launching an attack from the Continent. Aircraft taking part from

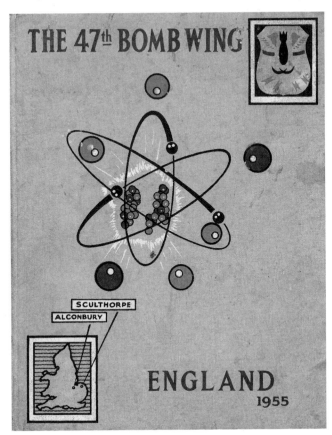

1955 Yearbook. Alconbury had been designated a satellite station of Sculthorpe during 1955.

420th Air Refuelling Sqn. (Fakenham Museum of Gas and Local History/Jim Baldwin)

the 49th Air Division included the B-45s, RB-45s and the F-84s. Targets were listed according to the possible Soviet priorities of the destruction of bomber bases and major population centres, attacks on ports and the air defence system.[11]

Within days of the end of the exercise a new unit arrived at Sculthorpe, the 420th Air Refuelling Squadron from Alexandria Air Force Base (later renamed England AFB), Louisiana, commanded by Major James B. Young. This was the first Tactical Air Command refuelling squadron to provide independent air-refuelling capacity within the 49th Air Division. Initially equipped with the older tankers, KB-29s, the squadron later upgraded to KB-50J tanker aircraft, with the main task of providing air-to-air refuelling for the nuclear-capable F-84 fighter-bombers.

AT THE CONTROLS OF THE B-45

Earlier that year, in March 1955, in a further loosening of the secrecy surrounding the base at Sculthorpe, the US Air Force headquarters in Washington DC granted permission to a *Flight* magazine journalist, C.M. Lambert, to fly in the cockpit of a B-45. This apparently was only the second time a non-combatant had been permitted to fly in an American jet bomber, and the first in a B-45.

Photography was permitted and a detailed description of the experience appeared in *Flight* magazine on 22 April 1955.[12] 'The B-45 is still, despite its age, a most interesting aircraft […] Generous facilities were granted by USAF headquarters in Washington to take air-to-air photographs' (from an accompanying Lockheed T-33). After a flight of 1 hour 40 minutes in the hands of Major H.J. McGee and crew, Lambert summed up his impressions: 'This was the end of a most enjoyable trip, and I was only sorry that the visibility from the back seat was not good enough for me to try a take-off and landing myself.'

Major McGee had completed his 1,000 hours on the B-45. C.M. Lambert's first thought after the flight was to head for 'one of the most gratefully downed whiskies of my life'.

While the service record of the B-45 had been outstanding, the aircraft was, by 1955, considered to be showing its age. Comparisons were being made with the latest generation of bombers with greater carrying capacity and speed along with higher operational ceilings, like the Boeing B-47 Stratojet medium bomber, which had entered service in 1951, and the Douglas B-66 Destroyer, first flown in 1954. The Martin B-57 Canberra was also on the list. The B-45 had suffered a number of accidents, but these was not necessarily related to the age of the aircraft, which was considered to be doing its job well. Discussions began at the highest level in Washington to choose a replacement aircraft but it took another two years before the B-45 was finally withdrawn from front-line service.

DISASTER STRIKES

On Friday 9 December 1955, an F-84F Thunderstreak (serial 52-6692) of the 55th Fighter-Bomber Squadron took off from Sculthorpe on an instrument training flight with 24-year-old Lieutenant Roy G. Evans at the controls. The squadron had been based at Sculthorpe since the previous August, arriving from Wethersfield, home of the parent unit, 20th Fighter-Bomber Wing. The atomic capable F-84F was one of the latest additions to the armoury of the 49th Air Division in England.

As the aircraft neared the Derbyshire border at 3,500ft, the pilot experienced a 'flameout', and after several failed attempts to restart the engine, was forced to bail out, landing safely in the Derbyshire moors. The pilotless aircraft drifted out of control and crashed into Lodge Moor Hospital on the outskirts of Sheffield, ploughing into a ward and causing the death of a female patient and injury to seven others. The *Daily Mirror* ran the headline 'Secret Jet hits Hospital' the next day and described the havoc of the aftermath. There was general relief because the tragedy could have been very much worse, as the aircraft had come to rest 10 yards from an ambulance station and a storage tank of 1,000 gallons of petrol. An immediate enquiry was convened by the Third Air Force, in what must have been a very black period for the 55th Squadron at Sculthorpe.

The Star, 10 Dec. 1955, Disaster at Lodge Moor Hospital, Sheffield. (Sheffield Newspapers Limited)

Daily Mirror

SAT DEC 10 1955

2ᴰ FORWARD WITH THE PEOPLE
No. 16,174

SECRET JET HITS HOSPITAL

One patient dies, seven are hurt

A faster-than-sound "Thunderstreak" of the type which crashed into the hospital

DAILY MIRROR REPORTERS

A PILOTLESS AMERICAN AIR FORCE JET FIGHTER CRASHED INTO THE MIDDLE OF A HOSPITAL YESTERDAY AND BURST INTO FLAMES.

The jet ploughed into a ward, through a corridor, into a second ward, and ended up on a lawn, facing the hospital mortuary.

As the plane blazed, ammunition in its wings began to explode.

But by a miracle only one patient—a forty-five-year-old woman—was killed.

Seven other patients, three of them children and four women, were injured.

THE HOSPITAL is the Lodge Moor Isolation Hospital, on the moors near Sheffield, Yorks.

THE DEAD WOMAN was Mrs. Elsie Murdoch, a mother of five, of Southroad, Sheffield. She was to have been released from hospital on Monday.

THE PLANE was a secret faster - than - sound F-84 "Thunderstreak" based at Sculthorpe, Norfolk.

THE PILOT, Lieutenant Roy G Evans, 24, baled out at 3,500ft. and landed unharmed on the side of Man Tor—the Shivering Mountain "—in Derbyshire, six miles from the hospital.

The crash drama began shortly before five o'clock over the Irish Sea.

The jet, apparently in trouble, streaked over the waves, at less than 200ft. and flashed across mistshrouded Ronaldsway Airport in the Isle of Man.

'Short of Fuel'

Lifeboats were launched in a gale in case the plane came down in the sea.

Minutes later the American Air Force control tower at Burtonwood, Lancs. picked up weak radio signals from the Thunderstreak's pilot.

"Short of fuel and

climbing," came the message.

Tensely the control tower staff waited as the pilot fought to gain sufficient height to allow him to bale out.

Then came the final message from the pilot:

"No fuel—baling out."

After Tea

In the hospital it was just after tea-time. The staff were clearing away the tea things . . . the patients were settling back for the evening . . .

Then, from out of the skies, the jet burst among the wards.

There was no warning —the jet's engine had cut out and it plunged silently to earth.

The jet hit the north block of the 465-bed hospi-

tal. It tore through North Ward 1, where there were twelve patients in cubicles.

Then it ripped along a 200ft. corridor and into North Ward 2, where there were fourteen patients, also in cubicles.

A number of patients were trapped as walls caved in on them.

Running a gauntlet of exploding ammunition, hospital staff members rushed to free the patients. But with the exception of the woman who died none was seriously injured.

Meanwhile, the flaming wreckage had started a number of small fires.

But firemen from Sheffield soon got the flames under control.

A male hospital orderly said later: "I was in the ward at the time. There was a tremendous crash.

"A gaping hole appeared in one corner of the room and one of the

wheels whizzed past me. It missed me by inches."

Another male orderly told how he crawled with a fire appliance under a hail of bullets to try to put out the blaze.

'No Panic'

A hospital management official said that there was no panic when the plane struck.

"All the patients behaved wonderfully in the circumstances," he said.

Later senior American Air Force officers arrived on the scene in four cars.

Then a squad of American Air Force police arrived to stand guard on the wreckage of the secret jet.

"They will stand guard all night," said Colonel Harold Bailer, operations officer of the U.S. base at Burtonwood.

The jet pilot, Lieutenant Roy Evans (right), with another American airman.

PILOT ESCAPES

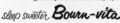
Daily Mirror report of Lodge Moor disaster, 10 Dec. 1955. (*Daily Mirror*)

The start of the new year, 1956, brought another tragedy for the base when a B-45 (serial 47-059) of the 84th Bomb Squadron crashed on its landing approach to RAF Lakenheath on 30 January. The snowy weather and poor visibility may have contributed to the accident in which only one crew member survived, Sergeant John Butts, tail gunner. The three members of the crew who died, Captain George W. Duncan (pilot), Captain John Murray (co-pilot) and 1st Lieutenant John O'Mahoney, are today commemorated in a memorial in the Green Park Social Centre, Sculthorpe.

1956 AND CHANGE AT THE TOP

The Whitsun holiday, Saturday 19 May 1956, was the occasion for another US Armed Forces 'At Home' day at Sculthorpe. Each year these events were becoming more popular, with well over the previous record of 20,000 people attending. The theme for the year was 'Partners for Peace', perhaps as a reminder of the disastrous floods of 1953 and the help the Americans had supplied. The massive 'shop window' of military aircraft included the RB-45 and B-45 Tornados, the T-33 and C-47, and from Upper Heyford the B-47E Stratojet of the 97th Bombardment Wing. A KB-29P Superfortress tanker attached to the 47th Wing equipped with all the latest technology and a Hawker Hunter from West Raynham were among several of the latest types on show to the public.

Earlier that month, the Republic F-84F Thunderstreaks of the 78th Fighter-Bomber Squadron flew in from Shepherds Grove while runway repair was in hand at the squadron's home base, in a stay that would last for twelve months. In July there was a rationalisation in the command structure when the administrative functions of the 49th Air Division were transferred to headquarters, Third Air Force, in the interests of greater economy and efficiency, and the division was disbanded at Sculthorpe. This made little difference to the operations of the 47th Air Wing but it proved the end of an era at Sculthorpe.

Mutual suspicion and fear between the nations showed little sign of easing. If anything, tension had moved up a gear with the formation of the Warsaw Pact, bringing together the USSR and its allies in a military alliance, during 1955. NATO had been stiffened by the admission of West Germany the same year. At the same time, there was an attempt to establish some dialogue between the powers in the first of the Four-Power Summits (USA, USSR, UK and France) in July 1955.

In spite of a goodwill visit by Soviet leaders Khrushchev and Bulganin to Britain in April 1956, which included a stopover at RAF Marham, the events of that year offered a reminder of the many tensions that existed in international relations. October 1956 had seen the ruthless crushing by the Soviet Union of the Hungarian uprising. The Suez Crisis of November, in which Colonel Nasser of Egypt had nationalised the

KB-29 of 420th Air Refuelling Sqn, May 1956. (Mike Hooks)

Another visitor – Fairchild C-123 Provider of 322 Air Division during 1956–8, when the aircraft operated in the division. Based in France. (V. Grimes)

Republic F-84F Thunderstreak being refuelled by KB-29P c. 1955/56. (M. J. F. Bowyer)

F-84F Thunderstreak FS-819 of the 78th Fighter-Bomber Sqn based at Shepherds Grove, Suffolk. The aircraft crashed at Thrandeston near Diss on 26 June 1958 and the pilot was killed. (David Whitaker)

Photo taken of the base from 1,500ft, August 1956. Control Tower in foreground. (David Whitaker)

Suez Canal and provoked Anglo-French and Israeli military intervention, caused a brief upset in Anglo-US relationships but little changed in the confrontation between East and West in the Cold War.

NOTES

1. Jackson, R., *Strike Force: The USAF in Britain since 1948,* p.84.
2. Info from Flt Sgt Mark Service, Squadron Historian, 67th Special Operations Squadron.
3. Jackson, p.62.
4. Fredriksen, J.C., *The B-45 Tornado,* p.128.
5. The Americans had rejected British style coal stoves in favour of their own systems, for efficiency and to avoid respiratory infections and diseases. (Jackson, p.55).
6. *Daily Mail,* 14 Dec. 1954.
7. Ibid. 13 Dec. 1954.
8. Ibid. 18 Dec. 1954.
9. Samuel, Wolfgang W.E., *Coming to Colorado: A Young Immigrant's Journey to become an American Flyer,* (Univ. of Mississippi Press, 2006) pp.234–42.
10. Ibid. pp.245–6.
11. Bowyer, M.J.F., *Force for Freedom, the USAF in the UK since 1948,* pp.108–9.
12. Flightglobal Archive, 22 April 1955 pp.523–5.

12. LIFE ON AND OFF BASE

'Flying at Sculthorpe was fun, but the real fun was the night life off base.'

(Airman Robert Ganci, 19th Tactical Reconnaissance Squadron, 1958)

From its beginnings as a satellite airfield in 1943, Sculthorpe was to become one of the largest and most important nuclear bases in Britain. The *New York Times* ran a profile of the base on 10 June 1951, describing it as being:

three B-50 hours from Leningrad, four from Moscow, nine Russian bomber hours from New York, forty jet minutes from the nearest Soviet fighter field in East Germany and twelve jet minutes from the coast of France. It is a few hundred acres of flat not very beautiful and remote English countryside, to which has been added a two mile-long strip of concrete running through some barley fields and sugar-beet patches.

The article concluded by pointing out that recreation was limited in this backwater, or so it seemed to the New York journalists.

The basic infrastructure and amenities of the base during the late 1940s and 1950s gave the appearance of not keeping pace with its operational activities. There had been much progress during the later 1940s when development resumed on the base as a Very Heavy Bomber (VHB) airfield. For single airmen the new barrack blocks (the 'Z' dorms) were completed by 1950, along with married quarters originally built for RAF occupation, but this was inadequate for the expansion that was about to come. The contrast with home bases in the USA must have been a stark one. If there was no space in the barrack blocks, single airmen had to tough it out in more basic accommodation. Typical was the experience of one airman of the 1st Aviation Field Depot Squadron on TDY from RAF Upper Heyford in 1951, who endured the winter in a rusty old Nissen hut. One of the problems was that until around 1952 most of the units coming and going had been in temporary occupation (TDY), which meant that there was little incentive to improve the infrastructure of the base.

Airman Third Class Wolfgang Samuel was struck by the temporary look of everything in the mid-1950s on his first overseas assignment. What stood out were 'the flimsy barrack-like structures with corrugated metal roofs and Quonset huts'. The only identifying feature of the Quonset hut, which served as a chapel, was the large cross above the door. His overall impression was that 'if any money was spent on this barren airfield it was on the concrete runways and ramps and on the aircraft hangars, certainly not on the facilities which served the men and their families'.[1] Even in the mid-1950s the Base Exchange (BX), like the commissary, was a rusty Quonset hut 'big enough to sleep ten men'.[2]

It is not surprising that club life on the base assumed supreme importance, with the Officers' Club, the NCO Club (which reputedly became one of the biggest and best throughout the USAFE), the Airmen's Club and the Wives' Club.

Accommodating single airmen on temporary duty was difficult enough but nothing compared to finding suitable quarters for married men and their families at a time when housing for local people was at a premium. The impact on local communities of building additional housing for the USAF was a matter of concern at government level as the Americans had a much higher standard of living than British people, especially in areas like East Anglia. There was also the factor that additional building land for the USAF might have to be obtained by compulsory purchase, which would further upset landowners and farmers who were still recovering from wartime disruption. There was no easy answer to the problem. In general it was felt that expansion within existing airfield boundaries was the best solution, although this was bound to take time.[3]

For many married airmen and their families there was no choice but to live off base, and assistance was provided in finding local accommodation – although the definition of 'local' could be a broad one, encompassing villages and towns as far afield as Cromer, Lowestoft and even Great Yarmouth. For obvious convenience, towns like Fakenham and villages like Sculthorpe, Docking and Syderstone were a favourite choice. Roger Lowe, a resident of Docking, remembered the Americans coming around knocking at doors asking for billets. His father, John, who owned a dairy business, had bought a large house in Docking called 'Swiss Villa' in the early 1950s and rented half of the house to an American service family. Roger was a boy at the time but recalled village life:

Americans were at Docking Hall, Holland House, North End Farm, North Farm, the Grange, Eton House, Mill House, our house and also the house over the road (now the antique shop). They were everywhere. They said Hunstanton was bumper to bumper with American cars. The hoteliers didn't worry about the tourists because they put the Americans up. They used to go as far as Cromer to billet. They thought nothing of travelling 20 or 30 miles. They were on base gas – their price, no rationing.

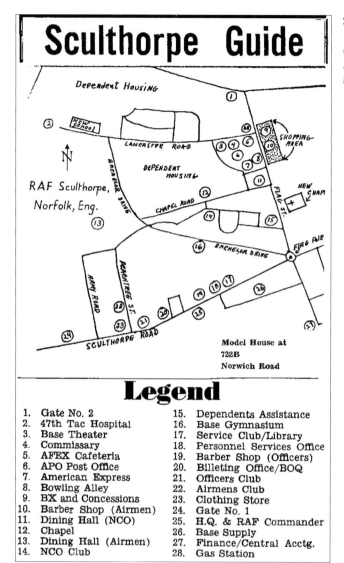

Sculthorpe Guide
1962 with Legend.
(from *Sculthorpe
Scanner* May 1962 –
Mrs Anne Manning)

Legend

1.	Gate No. 2	15.	Dependents Assistance
2.	47th Tac Hospital	16.	Base Gymnasium
3.	Base Theater	17.	Service Club/Library
4.	Commissary	18.	Personnel Services Office
5.	AFEX Cafeteria	19.	Barber Shop (Officers)
6.	APO Post Office	20.	Billeting Office/BOQ
7.	American Express	21.	Officers Club
8.	Bowling Alley	22.	Airmens Club
9.	BX and Concessions	23.	Clothing Store
10.	Barber Shop (Airmen)	24.	Gate No. 1
11.	Dining Hall (NCO)	25.	H.Q. & RAF Commander
12.	Chapel	26.	Base Supply
13.	Dining Hall (Airmen)	27.	Finance/Central Acctg.
14.	NCO Club	28.	Gas Station

Janet Duwe Ramsey from Wichita Falls, Texas, recalled her arrival at Syderstone from her home in Leicester as a young bride in October 1951. She had just married Sergeant Ronald Duwe of the air police who was based at Sculthorpe, and a penfriend from high school days. Unable to find any local housing, they rented a room in The Crown pub in Syderstone, or Syderville to some of the American airmen, as it sounded more like home. The first night they were tucked up in bed when, to their horror, another couple walked in as this was the only access to the adjoining room. Two days later, and much to their relief, they were able to rent some rooms in a house in Wells-next-the-Sea.[4]

In the early 1950s, many service families had no choice but to live in holiday-type chalets like those on South Beach Road, Hunstanton, with tragic consequences when the January 1953 floods hit the east coast. Even as late as the early 1960s, the only accommodation for some families was in a caravan site opposite the base hospital. Normally, airmen and their families were on a three-year posting and it was quite a complicated matter monitoring and assisting families arriving and leaving. At the start of 1958 there was quite an upheaval when the 47th Wing was re-equipping with a new aircraft, the B-66 Destroyer. To cope with the influx of new airmen and their families, the base took up the tenancy of an empty hotel in Cromer, the Newhaven Court Hotel, to provide stopgap accommodation until some of the resident families moved out of the base. Few of the families lodged there could have guessed at the hotel's illustrious past as a private house and retreat for such famous visitors as Oscar Wilde, Albert Einstein, Alfred Lord Tennyson and Ernest Shackleton. Sadly the hotel was destroyed by fire in January 1963.[5]

Off-base accommodation could mean anything from mansion houses, large country manors like Docking Hall and Cranmer Hall, Sculthorpe, to 'tiny cottages, heavily thatched and nestling in their incredibly profuse flower gardens, who now know the deep rumble of American exhaust pipes where before only the swish of bike tires [sic] was heard'.[6]

Twenty-year-old Airman Third Class Wolfgang Samuel had arrived at the base to join the 28th Weather Squadron in the early summer of 1955 and soon became determined to marry his American sweetheart, Harriet, and bring her to England. He had to work his way through the formalities, permission to marry from his commanding officer and parental permission from the parents (as both were under the age of 21). As a low ranker without a family, he was required to live on base, but as a married man he would be able to obtain authorisation to live in more congenial surroundings off base. One advantage was that he had just been promoted to airman second class, which brought his monthly pay and allowances to $240, and with the additional $4.50 per day to defray housing costs, his total income would rise to $400 per month. Bearing in mind that the dollar/pound sterling exchange rate was fixed at $2.80 to the pound, Wolfgang had every reason to believe he could comfortably support a wife, even one with expensive tastes. Accordingly he worked fast, ordering a Triumph TR-2, a red sports car, at a cost of $1,335, and then obtained from the base housing office a list of available off-base accommodation.

He was warned that finding suitable housing would be no easy task and so it proved. Living as far away as Norwich might have been the only option. He toured the Norfolk countryside, driving through Wells-next-the-Sea and then along Highway 149 [sic], eventually ending up at Stiffkey. Here he approached an old house which was up a track, in a courtyard with an iron gate leading to the front of the house. Previous occupants had included an air force captain and his family. The owners of the property, a retired Indian Army colonel and his wife, were at first unimpressed by the idea of an ordinary airman as a tenant rather than a commissioned officer. However in due course they relented and after Wolfgang and his new wife moved in, they all became the best of friends. For Wolfgang it was an introduction to a completely fresh experience of the life of the Norfolk landed gentry.[7]

After a brief transfer to London, Wolfgang finally left the 28th Weather Squadron at the end of April 1958 and returned to the United States and discharge from the air force. However, he enrolled in the Air Force Reserve Officer Training Corps (ROTC) and graduated in 1960, being commissioned as a second lieutenant. Thereafter he achieved his lifelong ambition of reaching aircrew status by qualifying as a navigator. He went on to serve with great distinction in Vietnam and subsequent postings until retiring as a colonel in 1985. In recent years he has been able to devote himself to family life and writing.

It must have been quite a logistical problem for the base commanders, to have personnel spread around a large rural county, as a crisis could erupt at any moment. Verrall Grimes, who worked in the NCO Club during the 1950s, recalled such times:

> Sometimes there would be an alert, at any time day or night – and when that happened everyone went to the base immediately. Sometimes the aircraft actually took off, as if there was to be an attack on the Eastern bloc and then the mission would be aborted. They probably didn't know at the time if it was for real. No doubt the aircraft were bombed up and ready. The entire base was cleared of aircraft in a matter of minutes. It sometimes happened on a Club or dining-in night, at awkward times. If it was a Friday night I dread to think what state the guys were in! I remember seeing these guys coming through Docking from Hunstanton at full speed in the big American cars and jeeps on their way to the base.

Tragedy struck in late March 1960 when an elderly couple, Herbert and Rose Barnes, were hit by a car driven by a drunk American airman at 70mph in the village of Docking, on their way to a meeting of the Docking Good Friends' Club in the village institute. Ronald Joel Beseda had drunk at least 5½ pints of beer, plus wine, in Hunstanton and was rushing back to his Sculthorpe base when he lost control of his car and mowed down the elderly couple. They died instantly, to the immense shock of the couple's family and Docking residents. The tragedy was a particularly poignant one in that Herbert, formerly the local postman, had survived the horrors of the trenches in the First World War, and in the words of his grandson Ted Barnes: 'Here was a man who had endured machine guns, artillery shells and gas shells and had come through it all to be killed by a motor car and a beer bottle in his home village.'[8] Herbert and Rose had also both endured the loss and severe injury of siblings as a result of the war. Verrall Grimes remembered the accident in Docking that day and recalled that his own parents had a narrow escape as they lived nearby and had walked to their home at about the same time.

Beseda was arrested, convicted of driving while drunk and causing the death of the elderly couple and sentenced to two years' imprisonment. However, soon afterwards he was sent back to the United States.[9] Accidents did happen but such tragic incidents were rare, although it once again highlighted some of the tensions that could exist between local people and the Americans from bases like Sculthorpe.

The construction of the 'tobacco' or 'commodity' houses on the base began from about 1956–58 in an effort to relieve the housing problems (see Chapter Sixteen) and married officers and NCOs among the combat crews were moved in on a first priority basis. The original RAF quarters to the north and two semi-detached houses along the Syderstone Road were allocated to more senior officers. However, living off base continued to be a fact of life for many airmen and their families until the base began to run down.

The impact of the American presence was considerable. In a *Times* article of November 1960, it was reported that around 5,000 American dependants were living around the Sculthorpe area, of whom about 1,000 were in boarding houses, hotels and private houses in Hunstanton 'paying substantial rents', with many others living in Norwich and King's Lynn. It was estimated that £100,000 was spent every week by the Americans in the Sculthorpe area, most of it going into the tills of local traders and landlords.[10]

To a boy like Roger Lowe, growing up in Docking during the 1950s, the presence of the Americans was an eye-opener:

> They were a different culture to us. They dressed better. They were smarter and they were better off. We were still struggling. I had hand-me-downs. Things were tight in the '50s. At Christmas we didn't have much. We probably had a present that would cost a quid and that was it. The Americans used to buy us presents better than what our parents could afford. Father used to smoke and he would supply the coal for the house and the American lodgers would supply the tobacco because tobacco in England was expensive and we couldn't get it sometimes.

Roger and his brother Steven had the additional bonus of attending a vacation Bible School at the base during the summer holidays, thanks to friends they had in Docking. As they were the only English children attending, they joined the others in pledging allegiance every morning to the American flag! Both received a certificate of full attendance dated 21 August 1959, signed by the base chaplain, Captain Roy B. Johnston, who lived at North Farm, Docking, with his family.

School holidays provided a chance for local lads like Tony Nelson and his friends to cycle from North Creake to Sculthorpe and sit all day at the end of the runway watching the aircraft landing and taking off. Often the air police would come to check them out, only to give them chocolate and chewing gum. One of the KB-29 captains from the 420th Air Refuelling Squadron, Captain Joe Rowen, lived in North

Creake and would fly low over the village because his two children attended the school there.

Simon Thorpe was a schoolboy from Docking who was able to indulge his passion for sport thanks to his friendships at the base. His natural father was Airman (later Technical Sergeant) Kenneth Alexander from North Carolina, who had been based at Sculthorpe in the early 1950s but had left in 1953 or 1954. Simon made many friends at the base, including Sheldon Gross, an American civilian who ran the motor pool. The enthusiastic youngster was enrolled in the boys' baseball team – the All-Stars – in the early 1960s at the age of 10, which earned him a photograph in the local newspaper. At the end of afternoon school in Docking he would don his full baseball gear, much to the disapproval of the head teacher, and wait to be picked up to go to the base. He took full advantage of other facilities on offer: .22 shooting, ten-pin bowling in the cafeteria, archery and weightlifting. He recalled a visit to the base by the Harlem Globetrotters.

Every kind of sport was catered for on the base: basketball, baseball, football and golf. There was a Rod and Gun Club but the stricter firearms laws in the UK and the control of hunting and fishing rights by landowners had to be adhered to. It came as a surprise that the police in England were unarmed.

KB-29P (serial 0-484120) of the 420th Air Refuelling Sqn, 1956. Note the long refuelling boom. The letter 'O' signified 'obsolescence', which applied to many older aircraft by the mid-1950s. Captain Joe Rowen (extreme left of picture) and his crew. Capt. Rowen lived in North Creake and two of his children attended the school there. (Tony Nelson)

Same aircraft, same crew. KB-29 of the 420th ARS. Captain Joe Rowen standing, extreme left. (Tony Nelson)

Much of the life of the base revolved around the clubs: the Officers' Club, the NCO Club and the Airmen's Club. Verrall Grimes worked in the NCO Club and recalled some of the big bands visiting: Stan Kenton, Ted Heath and the singers June Christy and Sarah Vaughan. Cleo Laine and Johnny Dankworth made appearances. On at least one occasion, Verrall was given the task of acting as Cleo's 'minder' for the night, helping to set up the band equipment and supplying food and drink when required. He earned £2 for his efforts.

Other stars of the 1950s included the singer Lita Roza, the bandleader Stanley Black, Dickie Valentine, Joe Loss and Jayne Mansfield, 'who turned up complete with sun tan and form-fitting knitted dress'.[11] On a more serious note, other visitors to the base included the Duke of Edinburgh and leading American politicians. On one occasion, the famous test pilot Neville Duke performed a flying display, probably during one of the open days.

Thanksgiving Day, traditionally held on the fourth Thursday of November, was an occasion for great celebrations and a holiday like Christmas. Other special events included St Patrick's Day and Labor Day. If there was a Hawaii Night, a supply of grass skirts and fresh fruit would be flown in from Hawaii. On one occasion a giant pumpkin was brought from Virginia for Verrall. Invitations would sometimes be extended to local people, locally based army regiments or nearby RAF Stations to share in the celebrations. At Christmas time, parties would be laid on for local children and the elderly.

Simon Thorpe with an airman at the base with a KB-50 of the 420th Air Refuelling Sqn. c. 1964. (Simon Thorpe)

Docking boy is Sculthorpe baseball star

Simon Thorpe

TEN-YEAR-OLD Simon Thorpe, of 9, Bradmere Lane, Docking, is a boy who prefers baseball to cricket and has made quick strides in the American national game.

Introduced to the sport by an American civilian living at Docking, Simon figured regularly last summer in the Yankees' team for his age group (9-12) at Sculthorpe base.

The Americans run a number of teams and leagues for young players and schoolboys. From these teams an "All Star" side is picked to represent the base in a series of games.

To his surprise Simon found himself picked for the "All Stars" side but then it was discovered he was not old enough. His American friends, however, presented him with a token in the shape of a baseball player as a consolation.

Simon as baseball star. (Simon Thorpe)

Money used on the base was special military currency called 'Scrip', which could only be exchanged at the base for English pounds or US dollars – it was a sort of 'mickey-mouse currency' but suited most servicemen as they tended to use the PX and the shops and clubs on the base rather than outside facilities. However, the rules were sometimes bent to pay taxi drivers in scrip as long as they were able to find a way of changing it back to English pounds. On occasions, there was a quiet illegal trade between some Norwich pub owners and airmen who would accept payment in scrip at a discount and later manage to exchange the scrip for pounds, once again at a discount!

The pubs and clubs around Norfolk were a big attraction for off-duty airmen. In the early 1950s, radar technician Staff Sergeant Donald Hall, who had joined the 84th Bomb Squadron in May 1952, ran a charter bus to Norwich every night and to London and back at weekends, until the Counties bus service objected to the competition. After fifty-eight years he still remembers the pub scene in Norwich and the singing of raucous songs like 'Knees Up Mother Brown'.[12] Don was a member of the Sculthorpe darts team and claims to have lost many matches and drunk much beer. During daytime leisure hours, he was a member of the Brancaster Golf Club and many times would hitch-hike from Sculthorpe to Brancaster and back – 'I met some real characters that way!' He left Sculthorpe on 9 August 1954 and on return to the United States was discharged from the air force after four years' service. Two months later he married his American sweetheart. The couple now live in Mill Creek, Washington, a suburb of Seattle.

Airman Robert Ganci was a gunner in the 19th Tactical Reconnaissance Squadron based at Sculthorpe in 1958, and at 19 years old, 'between my base pay, overseas pay, flight pay, separate rations and TDY money I was making more money than I ever had before in my life.' In his opinion, flying was fun but the real fun was the nightlife off base at the Palm Court pub in King's Lynn, which attracted 'beautiful young English girls from all the small towns and villages nearby'. Great Yarmouth at weekends did not allow the 47th Air Police to enforce the law as they did in King's Lynn and much enjoyment was to be had there. Robert Ganci

JOHNNY DANKWORTH
2 DENMARK PLACE, LONDON W.C.2

General Hawdy at Sculthorpe | Duke of Edinburgh inspects B-45 during his visit to Sculthorpe | Secretary of Defense Wilkison congratulates Neville Duke after his sound-barrier cracking flight

VIP visits, the Duke of Edinburgh and Neville Duke, test pilot. (1953 Pictorial)

84th Bomb Sqn Darts Team 'doing what we did best – drinking!' Don Hall is second from left. (Donald Hall)

maintains that one reason for the 19th being posted to Germany was that they were having too much fun in England.[13]

Apart from providing security at the base, the other function of the 47th Air Police was to patrol the towns and deal with any drunkenness and disorder. If there was any trouble in the villages or towns the air police would arrive and the offenders were unceremoniously thrown into the back of a truck and returned to the base.

Although racial segregation in the American armed forces had ended in 1948, there was some way to go before black soldiers and airmen were accepted on a fully equal basis with whites. The struggle for civil rights was at its height during the 1950s and early 1960s, especially in the southern states of the USA. Even in the NCO Club there could be tensions and resentment between the races, as Verrall Grimes occasionally noticed:

> I made it clear that everybody was equal in my eyes. There was still some separation between the races. They would sit at separate tables. There were some fights at the Club – dining-in nights sometimes. The coloured guys would bring in white girl friends – bussed in from Wisbech, Norwich, etc. – and they used to buy drinks for the girls and after a drink or two there would sometimes be trouble. They would sometimes have black and white 'custodians' at the Club to help sort out problems or disputes. I was friendly with the Master Sergeant who was in charge of the Club and we would go off and drive around the base, the Sergeant with a bottle of whisky and the odd tipple on the way. He was black. Some black guys rose in the ranks.

Hundreds of civilians were employed at the base, mostly on better pay rates than could be offered in equivalent jobs locally, in the NCO Club, as office workers, cleaners, drivers and suppliers of food and drink. The Docking firm of Waggs the Bakers was contracted to make bread and deliver it. Jenny Campling's father was a baker and confectioner at North and South Creake in the late 1940s and early 1950s and 'he used to go to the base night and mornings to deliver all sorts of bakery products, especially doughnuts, which the Americans loved. He would tour the peri-track'. The family adored the Americans – they were all so friendly, and when Jenny went into nurse training she recalled that she was the only one with nylons and a petticoat – they were so generous.'[14]

Community relations were of vital importance to the smooth running of the American bases and any potential problems were taken seriously by the air force authorities. The road closures and fresh road building around Sculthorpe and Syderstone were still a sensitive issue. There was a report in *The Times* in October 1956 that Colonel J.F. Harris, base commander at Sculthorpe, was appealing to American airmen to approach house rent tribunals for rent reductions as a last rather than a first resort, for the benefit of good Anglo-American relations. On a more raunchy note, as reported by the *Eastern Daily Press* in December 1957, the US Third Air Force authorities promised a full investigation into reports that some American airmen based at Sculthorpe and Alconbury were posing as 'ranch hands', setting up 'weekend camps' in a remote part of Nottinghamshire and luring teenage girls to parties. One farmer reported a long queue of taxis from Nottingham waiting to drive up a narrow lane near his farm!

Mrs K. Bygrave of Hethersett recalls living in Sculthorpe in the late 1950s and being much in demand as a babysitter for American families. On one occasion she answered a knock on her employer's door and was faced with the sight of a certain captain of the air police pointing a gun at her chest. He looked tired and emotional and said he was looking for his wife, 'who was messing with one of your local goddamned cow-hands'. She quietly explained that he must have gone to the wrong house so he lowered his gun and went away. He was later sent back to the United States.[15]

In the course of the 1950s and 1960s, there were thousands of marriages between American airmen and English girls. Many of these took place in local churches. A typical example was the wedding of Staff Sergeant Jewel M. 'Nip' Smart of the 47th Bomb Wing to Noreen Powers, which took place in St Mary's Church, Earlham, in November 1954. 'Nip' belonged to the 47th Medical Group and had assisted in the flood disaster of January 1953 (see Chapter Ten). The couple returned to the United States where 'Nip' was at first discharged from the air force and then re-enlisted, eventually retiring as a chief master sergeant after twenty-seven years' service. They remained happily married until Noreen's death in 2008. Today 'Nip' lives in Bossier City, Louisiana, where he plays golf three times a week and enjoys travelling.

Sergeant Bill Tollefson of the 9th Air Rescue Squadron arrived in Sculthorpe in August 1951 and met his future wife Jean in the NCO Club after she had hitched a lift to the base with a band from Cromer. They continued to meet throughout Bill's time in Sculthorpe and she joined him in the United States in August 1953, a few months after he had left England for Randolph Air Force Base, San Antonio, Texas,

where they married. Bill was discharged from the air force in December 1953 and joined a manufacturing company building electric vehicles. The couple now live in Rockford, Illinois.

Donald Aspinall had joined the 47th Air Police at Sculthorpe at the end of May 1952 after serving in the Korean War (see Chapter Nine), and it was in England that he met Anne, his future wife, but only after leaving Sculthorpe for RAF Sealand in Flintshire. She was from Heswall in Cheshire, and they married in 1956, although they were not together long as she died a few years later of leukaemia.

Unexpected visitor for Mrs Bygrave. (Mrs K. Bygrave)

'Nip' Smart and Noreen's wedding at Earlham, Norwich, 6 November 1954. (Jewel M. 'Nip' Smart)

'Nip' Smart and his wife Noreen, Sculthorpe, 1954. (Jewel M. 'Nip' Smart)

There was a brief return to Sculthorpe, living off base in Hunstanton. In the meantime, Donald's work had changed to computer programming and he worked in the UK for several years until returning to the United States to work at the Pentagon. He retired from the air force in 1970 after twenty-three years' service and today lives with his present wife (and cat) in Toano, near Williamsburg, Virginia.

For some other couples the adjustments required were too great to cope with. However, in the three years prior to 1960 about 3,000 marriages had taken place in the UK between American servicemen and British girls. At the start of 1961, it was estimated that at Sculthorpe, upwards of twenty marriage ceremonies per month were taking place between American airmen and English brides. For this reason the USAF authorities requested that the new all-denominational American Chapel (Building 546), completed in 1960, be registered for the solemnisation of marriages

Z blocks in the 1980s. (Richard Jermy)

Z blocks in 2013. (Author)

Former American chapel in 2013 (now industrial use). (Author)

under the Worship Registration Act of 1855. The request was granted, to the convenience of personnel who otherwise had to travel to Mildenhall or seek the help of local churches.[16]

NOTES

1. Samuel, Wolfgang W.E. (later Col. USAF ret'd), *Glory Days: The Untold Story of the Men who Flew the B-66 Destroyer* (Schiffer Military History 2008), p.61.
2. *1957 in England.*
3. Memo by Sec. of State for Air (CAB/129/57), 24 Nov. 1952.
4. Ramsey, Janet, quoted on the Francis Frith website and email to author, 14/04/2012.
5. *Eastern Daily Press,* 23 Jan. 1963 and 23 Jan. 2013.
6. *1957 in England.*
7. Samuel, Wolfgang W.E., *Coming to Colorado* (Univ. Press of Mississippi 2006), Chap. 21 and 22.
8. Barnes, Ted, quoted by Steve Snelling in *Eastern Daily Press Weekend,* 'Tribute to my brave Grandad', 9 March 2013.
9. I am grateful to Ted Barnes for information about the tragedy involving his grandparents.
10. *The Times,* 17 Nov. 1960.
11. *1957 in England.*
12. Don Hall requested the words of the song again, to impress his American friends. The author obliged!
13. Quoted in Samuel, Wolfgang W.E., *Glory Days,* p.78.
14. Jenny Campling, interview with author, Dec. 2011.
15. Letter from Mrs K. Bygrave to author, 29 Dec. 2011.
16. AIR 2/16109. Letter, RAF Sculthorpe to Sec. of State for Air, 'RAF Sculthorpe Chapel No. 1'.

13. FRESH HORIZONS (1957–60)

'Sculthorpe: Base with Personality.'

The Stars and Stripes

The year 1957 ushered in a new age of ballistic missiles, which would eventually make the conventional bomber, armed with the free-fall bomb, redundant. As early as 1952 there had been talk of the 'guided bomb' – the forerunner of 'smart' bombs of today. American and Soviet scientists had been working on missile delivery systems for many years, originally pioneered by the Germans with the V2 rocket in the Second World War. The Soviets succeeded in launching their first intercontinental ballistic missile (ICBM) in August 1957, closely followed in October by the launch of *Sputnik I* – the world's first artificial satellite – an event which many regard as the start of the space race. It was a short step from this to arm ICBMs with atomic warheads, inaugurating a new nuclear arms race.

In the meantime, the backbone of the UK-based tactical nuclear forces continued to be the 47th Bomb Wing at Sculthorpe combined with the two other USAF fighter-bomber wings, the 20th FBW at Wethersfield and the 81st at Bentwaters. Strategic Air Command (SAC) continued to rotate its bombers, the latest example being the B-47 Stratojet strategic bomber, at various bases in the UK and other parts of Europe. This force was now being stiffened by the Royal Air Force's V-bomber force, comprising the Vickers Valiant and the Avro Vulcan already in service, with the Handley Page Victor arriving in November 1957. Within twelve months, RAF Thor ICBMs would be in place at Feltwell in Norfolk, the first of an eventual total of twenty launch sites for the missiles in East Anglia and Yorkshire.

OUT WITH THE OLD, IN WITH THE NEW

Much of this lay in the future. The experience of the Korean War had convinced the US Air Force of the need for a high performance day and night tactical bomber of superior capability to the existing B-45. The result was a contract awarded to Douglas for five preproduction Douglas RB-66A all-weather/night photo reconnaissance aircraft. The design was based on the US Navy's carrier-borne A3D Skywarrior, and the first flight of the new prototype took place in June 1954. With a crew of three, each with ejection seats, and powered by two Allison turbojets, the aircraft had a maximum speed of 631mph and a ceiling of nearly 40,000ft with a range of over 1,800 miles. This, together with a multiple camera installation and bombing and navigational radar, made the aircraft an ideal replacement for the now ageing RB-45 Tornado. Deliveries to the US Air Force began in February 1956 and plans were afoot to re-equip the photo reconnaissance units as soon as practicable.

In early January 1957, three modified Boeing KB-50D tankers joined the KB-29 tankers of the 420th Air Refuelling Squadron at Sculthorpe. These aircraft used the three-point 'probe and drogue' system favoured by the RAF rather than the boom refuelling method used by the KB-29s, the first of their type allocated to a unit in the US Air Forces in Europe (USAFE). In short, this would enable three F-84 fighter-bombers to be refuelled at the same time, assisted by the addition of four 500-US-gallon underwing tanks of the tanker aircraft. Tragedy struck the squadron on 2 February when two KB-29s collided at 15,000ft during a weekend training exercise near Saint-Lô in France, with the loss of thirteen airmen. A report stated that there was poor visibility, the lead aircraft lost speed and the second ploughed into it.

KB-29 of 420th Air Refuelling Sqn at Wethersfield, 15 June 1957. Note refuelling boom. (Mike Hooks)

KB-50D of 420th Air Refuelling Sqn at Wethersfield, 15 June 1957. (Mike Hooks)

By February, the first of the RB-66B Destroyers had been flown in to replace the RB-45s in the 19th Tactical Reconnaissance Squadron (TRS). The cover story for the transatlantic flight via the Azores was that the aircraft were mere B-26s and capable of only 460 knots.[1] The RB-66s were also equipped for in-flight refuelling, hence the timely arrival of the KB-50s, although it was considered unlikely that more than two RB-66s could be refuelled at any one time. It was no accident that that the new aircraft were prioritised for the 19th TRS and similar units within USAFE, as this role was key in the NATO requirement for continuous up-to-date reconnaissance for ground and air forces.

The early months of 1957 must have been a feast for airplane spotters at Sculthorpe, as testified by a visit of a *Flight* magazine journalist.[2] The airfield was a hive of activity and the range of aircraft included RB-66s, KB-29 and KB-50 tankers, B-45s of the 47th Bomb Wing and F-84Fs of the 81st Fighter-Bomber Wing, which were described as the 'world bombing champs'. There was also a motley collection of C-119s, C-47s, a couple of ageing B-26 target tugs, T-33s for training and a US Army H-21 helicopter.

RB-66B of 19th Tactical
Reconnaissance Sqn 1957.
Later served in Thailand.
(M.J.F. Bowyer)

RB-66 4421 of 19th Tactical Reconnaissance Sqn. This aircraft was at Sculthorpe from
Feb. 1957 to January 1959. On 14 December 1959 the aircraft crashed on approach to
Bruntingthorpe and all three crew were killed. (Mike Hooks)

RB-66 4421 of 19th Tactical Reconnaissance Sqn, c. 1957. (M. J. F. Bowyer)

RB-66 of 19th Tactical Reconnaissance Sqn. (David Whitaker)

RB-66 with KB-50 in refuelling mode. (David Whitaker)

RB-66 with KB-50 in refuelling mode. (David Whitaker)

KB-29P. (M. J. F. Bowyer)

Base directions signage c. 1957/58. Note 47th Bomb Wing sign on top. Sculthorpe was a busy place. (G. Wickstrum)

The main purpose of the *Flight* visit was to outline the role of the RB-66 'Night Photo Jet' of the 19th TRS, as this aircraft was an intriguing addition to the military line-up of that era. There was a special three-week crew familiarisation course followed by flight simulator training in Germany and a series of training flights until the crews reached operational standard. The RB-66 was described as 'quite a change' from the stately old RB-45, with its swept wings, single pilot's position, narrow track undercarriage and a large ribbon-type drag chute deployed at landings. Designed for night or day photography at high or low altitude, the structure was very strong. The main mission of the 19th TRS was low-level night photography, although the target was approached from high-level, a special technique being employed to locate a pinpoint target at low-level at night. Packed with the latest electronic devices for mapping, navigation and communications, the aircraft represented a major addition to the armoury of NATO.

The crews seemed to be well satisfied with the new aircraft, which they claimed could outrun any fighter except the Hunter. The conversion of crews to the new aircraft was said to be progressing well, as would have been expected of a squadron which had won the USAFE tactical squadron proficiency award on four occasions. Major John B. Anderson, squadron commander, summed up his impressions of the changes to *The Stars and Stripes*, official newspaper of the American Armed Forces, in an article entitled 'Sculthorpe: Base with Personality': 'I never knew that I'd be responsible for $20 million worth of equipment.'

When the conversion was completed, twenty of the aircraft were expected to be skimming the skies over Norfolk. 'England's country lanes and thatched roofs blur between the aircraft's pods and swept wings – fixed only in history and the camera eye as the 19th sends forth its missions night and day as one of NATO's northern scouts.'[3]

Open Day with Z blocks in background. (G. Wickstrum)

Line-up on typical Open Day, KB-50, RAF Hastings and Canberra. (Richard Jermy)

Armed Forces Day in May 1957 followed the usual pattern of an open day at Sculthorpe, but this year with a difference, as it was the tenth birthday of the US Air Force 'as a separate member of the land–sea–air defence team – and our 50th birthday as the Nation's specialists in airpower [...] From a three man organization in 1907, it has developed to a force with power to hold peace for America, or to cope with global war or limited aggression.'[4]

C-119 Flying Boxcar, probably for spare parts. (G. Wickstrum)

Another open day visitor – Boeing C-97 Stratofreighter. (Richard Jermy)

Open day visitor, late 1950s. F-84F of 166th Fighter Sqn Ohio Air National Guard based at Lockbourne AFB. This aircraft crashed at Baer Field, Indiana, on 15 May 1965 and the pilot was killed. (V. Grimes)

Hawker Hunter warming up for take-off on an open day, 1957. (David Whitaker)

The B-45 Tornados of the 47th Bomb Wing were showing their age, although the Wing had performed with great distinction over the years. By now, they were a common sight in the skies over Norfolk. Roger Lowe recalled his boss at East Rudham Garage calling them the 'smokey joes', as they left a dense black trail. On a typical day one would be taking off every minute and this would continue for half or three-quarters of an hour.[5]

One of the 'smokey joes' (B-45s) taking off. (M.J.F. Bowyer)

B-45 formation. (David Whitaker)

This record of service came at a high cost as there had been between thirty and forty B-45 and RB-45 accidents since the units had arrived in Norfolk, several of them fatal. Typical of this was the crash near RAF West Raynham of B-45 (serial 07-083) on 20 September 1957 during a training flight. The pilot, Major Torino V. DiSalvo, 84th Squadron commander, and all his crew perished.

B-45 of 84th Bomb Sqn c. 1957. Note 84th Bomb Sqn insignia on external fuel pod. (Mike Hooks)

B-45 on maintenance. (G. Wickstrum)

B-66 dispersal area. (M.J.F. Bowyer)

B-45 054, 47th Bomb Wing. Withdrawn from operational use at Sculthorpe 25 June 1958. (G. Wickstrum)

B-45 091, 84th Bomb Sqn. Withdrawn from operational use at Sculthorpe 11 July 1958. (G. Wickstrum)

At the end of November 1957, it was announced that the B-66 Destroyer would replace the B-45 during the first half of 1958 in the 47th Bomb Wing. During January 1958, the first B-66s were flown to Sculthorpe via the Azores by crews drawn from the 34th Bomb Squadron, 17th Bomb Wing, based at Eglin Air Force Base. The 84th Bomb Squadron was the first to re-equip, followed closely by the 86th at Alconbury and finally the 85th at Sculthorpe. The B-45 finally ended its days there during the summer.

Parallel with this development was a further upgrading of the tanker fleet with the arrival of the modified KB-50J to the 420th Air Refuelling Squadron, equipped with an additional 700 US-gallon fuel tank and two jet engine pods to facilitate the refuelling of the faster B-66s.[6] There was a lucky escape for the seven-man crew of a KB-50 (it was not specified which version) on 6 December when the aircraft caught fire on landing just after 11 p.m. The airfield fire crews leapt into action and brought the blaze under control without loss of life or severe damage. In order to calm local fears an official spokesman stated that 'No atom bombs were aboard', but the potential for a disaster was clear, as indicated by a question in Parliament the following March seeking information from the Secretary of State for Air as to which fire brigades attended the crash. On this occasion, local civil brigades had not been summoned.[7]

On occasions the crews of the KB-50s were unable to retract the refuelling hoses in-flight and had to land with the hoses dangling, creating a massive fire and explosion risk. The 'Big Red Trucks' of the fire department had to go into action immediately, red lights blinking, in hot pursuit of the aircraft as it landed, one by the right wing and one by the left until the aircraft stopped in the middle of the runway. Jerry Roth, stationed at the base from 1956 until 1959, recalled that 'in the late '50s all of the flight line mechanics had a great deal of respect for the guys in the fire department. The boys in the "Big Red Trucks" would answer the call 24/7 with spectacular exuberance'.

TEETHING PROBLEMS, AND WORSE

The B-66 was an efficient and effective aircraft and a considerable advance on the B-45, but there could be systems failures. A B-66 navigator who lodged with the Lowe family in Docking recalled how on many occasions the hydraulics failed on the undercarriage and the wheels had to be cranked down by hand.[8]

On a much more serious note, failures could be fatal, as on 14 April 1958 when RB-66 (serial 54-0422), of the 19th Tactical Reconnaissance Squadron, crashed on approach to the airfield near West Barsham Hall while attempting a blind landing during a training flight. The crew of three were all killed: Captain R.E. Taylor, 1st Lieutenant R.B. Handcock and B.M. Valencia. A local farm steward, Mr G. Skelton, described how the aircraft was losing height as it passed overhead, and exploded in the air. He ran to the scene but nothing could be done. The Fakenham fire brigade and fire-fighting teams from the airfield were called out but the crew were beyond help. Later, a US Air Force spokesman emphasised that the public were in no danger during the incident.

A serious incident on 13 June 1958 involving the 86th Bomb Squadron at Alconbury brought the sort of headlines least wanted by the US Air Force. An airman, 2nd Class Mechanic Vernon L. Morgan, with no flight training, in a fit of frustration, took off in a B-45 (serial 47-046), and shortly after take-off crashed onto the main Edinburgh to King's Cross railway line at Abbots Ripton, Cambridgeshire, and was killed. This must have been one of the last B-45 losses in England. The airman was one of eight killed that day in separate accidents, one involving a collision between an RAF Canberra from Wyton and a USAF T-33 Trainer from Alconbury and the other in Brigg, Lincolnshire, when a Canberra crashed, with the loss of the crew of three. These incidents fed the growing public concern about the rate of aircraft accidents in urban and semiurban areas.

These fears were heightened by a mishap on 3 July in which an RB-66B (54-433A), once again of the 19th Tactical Reconnaissance Squadron, encountered technical problems on a return flight to Sculthorpe from Spangdahlem Air Base, Germany. On approach to the home airfield, the pilot, Captain William A. Marcum, was unable to lower the wheels for landing owing to a leak in the hydraulic systems. The attempt to lower the undercarriage manually failed and the leak was so severe that there was no alternative for the crew but to eject from the aircraft after setting the autopilot. This must have been the incident recalled by local historian Jim Baldwin, who happened to be cycling to Snoring that day to see his girlfriend:

> I don't think I saw her after all, because on the way I heard 'pop', 'pop', 'pop' and looked up and saw three guys on parachutes with the B-66 still flying in what seemed like a straight line. I thought one of the aircrew was coming down in the field so I threw my bike against the hedge and ran towards him, but he was miles away although it looked like he was in the next field. They must have steered the aircraft on autopilot as it appeared to be heading out to sea.

All three crewmen ejected safely, but the aircraft flew on, turning to the left and made three or four circles about 5 miles in diameter, 7 miles to the north of the base. It then flew over the base and eventually ran out of fuel, crashing 27 miles away at Saxlingham Nethergate, 6 miles south of Norwich.

Bob Collis, aviation archaeologist and historian, was part of a group that recovered the wreckage in 2009. The remains, including the drogue parachute harness and pack, a fire axe, a roll of unexposed film and the compressed engine parts, were donated to Bentwaters Cold War Museum in Suffolk.[9]

A further tragedy occurred near St Vith, Belgium, on 13 August 1958, when a KB-50 tanker flying from Wiesbaden to Sculthorpe exploded and caught fire, with

RB-66 out of control and falling to earth, 3 July 1958. Computer-generated image by Kim Collinson. (Bob Collis)

the loss of all seven of the crew. The cause of the explosion was a mystery and an appeal went out for any witnesses to contact the Directorate of Flight Safety in the Air Ministry. An unidentified aircraft had been seen circling the area shortly after the accident.

NUCLEAR BUNKER INCIDENT

'Gentlemen, we have a problem' – words spoken by Air Force General B.C. Harrison in a classified meeting at the Pentagon in Washington during 1959, according to an article in *Mother Jones* magazine of November 1998 under the heading 'Who is Watching the People who are Watching the Nukes?'

The reference was to an incident at Sculthorpe on Thursday 30 October 1958 when a mentally deranged airman, Master Sergeant Leander V. Cunningham, locked himself in a building on the base, armed with a .45 pistol, and threatened to take his own life. For 8 hours, his wife, Nancy, along with chaplains, medical personnel and senior officers, talked with him; they eventually persuaded him to surrender and be taken into medical care. Sergeant Cunningham was a nuclear weapons technician of the 1st Tactical Depot Squadron, a unit with responsibility for the storage and mainte-nance of nuclear weapons at the base (see Chapter Seven).

The press had a field day and the story was widely reported. The Friday edition of the *Eastern Daily Press* ran the headline 'Norfolk Atom Base Drama' and *The Times* referred to a 'Deranged Sergeant at Bomber Base'. The US Air Force authorities at Ruislip, Middlesex, did their best to play down the affair as being purely a mental health breakdown of the man due to family worries, with no resulting injury or damage to property. Any suggestion that the man was in a nuclear arms store, let alone attempting to prime a weapon, was dismissed. The building in question was not identified but was described as 'an old parachute tower'. No doubt the US Air Force hoped that this would settle the matter.

But rumours were rife and refused to go away, if only because so many civilians worked at the base and could not easily be silenced. Verrall Grimes, who worked in the NCO Club, recalled the incident:

I remember when an American went berserk and locked himself into one of the bomb shelters, with a gun to prime one of the atomic weapons, and they had to close the base and nobody was allowed to leave any building until the situation was restored. They kept quiet about that.

The *Eastern Daily Press* reporter described the complete lockdown of the base for several hours and the experiences of 'several hundred Norfolk people' who worked at the base. One eyewitness described how he had been confined to a building for 2½ hours during the emergency and told to 'keep his head down' until curiosity overcame him he peeped out of the window and 'there was not a soul in sight except for the American police'. At the end of the afternoon, civilians were allowed to leave the base as usual and his impression was that there was an unusually large crush of vehicles trying to get off the base, which police were trying to control'. [10]

As rumours persisted, the *Eastern Daily Press* of 1 November reported that the US Air Force officially denied that there were any nuclear priming devices inside the building where the sergeant had locked himself up. Photographs had even been issued of the supposed building in question described as a 'training tower', some 30 feet high, surrounded by a wire fence and close to the perimeter track. It was said that the tower was several hundred yards from the area which was heavily guarded and encircled by dogs. The base information officer, Captain John W. Plantikow, must have been working long hours over the succeeding days dealing with the pressmen's questions and doubts.

As early as 5 November, Harold Davies, MP for the Leek division of Staffordshire, raised in Parliament the matter of the 'berserk American airman' and the question of the safety of nuclear weapons. In reply, George Ward, Secretary for Air, stated that 'it is impossible for one individual to set off a nuclear explosion [...] even assuming that he could get into the building, which I think would have been impossible'.

This did not prevent the appearance of nightmare scenarios in the popular press after the event reached public notice: 'Should the sick man's pistol shot somehow set off the nuclear package in the bomb, the base, the town, the countryside would be a mass of radioactive rubble.'

In reality it was unlikely that any nuclear explosion could have taken place, as the components necessary for this were stored in widely separated bunkers. At worst, the firing of a weapon might have detonated the high explosive required to trigger the nuclear device but not the device itself, but that in itself might have caused the deaths of people in the immediate area and very severe damage.

Official disclosure did not take place until 1962 that the sergeant had been intending to fire his weapon at a nuclear bomb and that he was suffering from some form of mental delusion. The delayed admission was just as well, as one American source admitted at the time that 'disclosure of the event would have knocked us out of England'. [11]

Even in 1962 the US authorities did not admit to any fissionable material being present in the building where the sergeant had locked himself in, although they could not deny that his intention was to detonate a nuclear device.

In December 1962, questions were raised in the House of Commons by two Labour Members of Parliament, Tom Driberg and Michael Foot, about the Sculthorpe incident and the question of the medical screening of those responsible for nuclear weapons. Only weeks after the Cuban missile crisis, Prime Minister Harold Macmillan had to provide the necessary assurances about this and the wider question of UK and US consultation over the use of nuclear weapons in any emergency. The prime minister repeated the American assurance that there was no fissionable material in the building but 'there was some explosive' and that 'it is just conceivable that he might have caused it to explode had he carried out his threat, which was to kill himself, not to shoot the explosive'.[12]

After 1962, the American authorities introduced a system of psychological screening of candidates for nuclear-sensitive jobs and a 'buddy' system by which nobody would ever be alone in a position where a mistake could be made without another person beside him to rectify it. The *Daily Mirror* put it more bluntly on 15 December 1962: 'US Clamp on A-Men – After the case of the atom-base maniac […] Tough new rules to guard America's atom bomb stocks from maniacs and other "unstable" people were announced yesterday.' These included a ban on people who drank too much alcohol or those who showed 'family or financial irresponsibility'.[13]

NUCLEAR ARMAGEDDON

The nuclear bunker incident highlighted the issue about the security of nuclear armouries, which has become even more of an anxiety today. The possibility of a Third World War, with its unthinkable consequences, had lurked in the background of everyday life since the advent of weapons of mass destruction. Nevil Shute's novel *On the Beach*, published in 1957 and produced as a film in 1959 starring Gregory Peck and Ava Gardner, was set in Australia following a Third World War in which the most of the world had been destroyed by nuclear fallout, with the destruction of human and animal life. It was against the background of the developing nuclear arms race that the Campaign for Nuclear Disarmament (CND) was formed in January 1958.

A more immediate fear was the possibility of a nuclear accident, caused by an aircraft crashing or some other malfunction at one of the bases. There had been a number of scares, but possibly the most worrying in East Anglia occurred on 27 July 1956 when a B-47 Stratojet was caught in a crosswind while landing at Lakenheath and careered out of control, crashing into the nuclear bomb dump and exploding in flames. The crew were killed and the resulting fire spread rapidly, but the nuclear igloo remained intact thanks to its heat and blast-resistant features. Even if the fire had engulfed the interior of the weapons store, a nuclear explosion would have been highly unlikely. At worst, the conventional high explosive would have detonated and this in itself would have been serious enough. The risk of nuclear fallout on this occasion was nil.

BUSINESS AS USUAL

Even at the height of the nuclear bunker incident, it was business as usual. The *Eastern Daily Press* of 3 November 1958 published a photograph of a collection of senior officers' headgear stacked in the cloakroom of the Officers' Club with the commentary: 'There were obviously plenty of high-ranking officers around when this photograph was taken at the USAF base at Sculthorpe, of a jumbled array of headgear, swagger sticks and canes tossed down by guests when they went into the Officers' Club for lunch.'[14]

The 19th Tactical Reconnaissance Squadron relocated to Spangdahlem in Germany on 10 January 1959 with their RB-66 Destroyers, leaving behind the two squadrons of the 47th Bomb Wing. The following August, the 86th Bomb Squadron returned to Sculthorpe from Alconbury to join its sister squadrons.

The lighter side of life featured on the weekend of 9–10 May 1959 when the British Women Pilots Association held their flying meeting at Little Snoring, including a dinner-dance in the USAF Officers' Club at Sculthorpe on the Saturday evening. Over the course of the weekend, the members had been treated to a flypast of a KB-50 tanker with three jet aircraft attached.

On a more dramatic note, KB-50 tanker aircraft from the 420th Air Refuelling Squadron participated in the record flight of two F-100 Super Sabres in August during Operation 'Julius Caesar', the first North Pole crossing between Britain and Alaska by jet fighters. These aircraft, among the latest supersonic tactical fighter-bombers based at Wethersfield, and nuclear capable, were refuelled by the KB-50s in the course of a flight of 5,405 miles lasting for 9 hours, 37 minutes. The objective was to demonstrate the ability of the US Air Force to deploy jet fighter fleets between Europe and the Far East.

There was a lucky escape for six crew of a KB-50 on 1 February 1960 when the aircraft's landing gear jammed during a routine training flight. All attempts at freeing the gear failed, and the pilot, Captain T.F. Rogenski, had no choice but to carry out a wheels-up crash landing. Three of the crew bailed out successfully and, after the aircraft had circled for a time to use up fuel, the pilot brought the aircraft in to a successful if dramatic touchdown. The full emergency had alerted the Fakenham Fire Brigade and the Fakenham police as well as the local RAF stations of West Raynham, North Pickenham and Watton.

LIFE ON THE FRONT LINE

The 86th Bomb Squadron rejoined its two stablemates, the 84th and 85th, at Sculthorpe in August 1959 and the three squadrons now shared the 'strip' alerts which had been regular feature of life at the base. Under the code name *Victor Alert,* six aircraft, two from each squadron, would be on 5-minute alert with weapons loaded and crews ready to go. The crews would be billeted by their B-66 Destroyers on the flight line for seven days at a time. One pilot who experienced these alerts was Don Harding (later lieutenant colonel USAF), who had recently joined the 84th Bomb Squadron at Sculthorpe.[15] He recalled that each aircraft bomb bay contained the Mark 5 atom bomb, which took up the entire space, and a separate canister, which held the ball of uranium, was brought out which had to be fitted by one of the crew into the bomb – 'You never lifted anything so heavy in your life.' The bomb itself was packed with TNT sticks surrounding it, each fitted with a detonator to cause the 'implosion' which would set off the chain reaction. The plan was for the bomb to be released at about 38,500ft, and arming would take place at 14,000ft. At the programmed height of 3,000ft the bomb would explode in an airburst. The technical issues involved meant that the crews had to undertake 6-monthly Bomb Commander's tests.

Eventually, the Mark 28 bomb was made available: a smaller weapon 2ft in diameter and 18ft long. The crews would punch in the settings for the yields required to a maximum of 1.1 megatons (equivalent to just over a million tons of TNT). Don Harding recalled that his preprogrammed targets were a Russian naval headquarters in one of the Baltic states and a secondary target at Katowicz (Katowice) airfield in Poland. The crews were aware that their chances of survival were slim even if they could get through to the target, as even at 38,000ft the blast would probably have been fatal.[16]

There was constant readiness, 24 hours a day and 7 days a week, but at the same time many hours of inactivity which had to be filled with games of bridge, reading, studying and even practising golf. Verrall Grimes, who worked in the NCO Club, remembered these alerts:

> When there was a big barbecue in the summer months we had to take out the food to the flight line. They crews had to stay with the aircraft at the hard standings and dispersals – the crews weren't allowed to leave the aircraft to come to the Club as they were on stand-by – this often happened during the Cold War.

The alerts would vary according to operational requirements. On occasions there would be a simulated alert when the bombs would be loaded, full cockpit checks carried out, then the ground crews would unload the bombs 'and then we would race as fast as we could to the end of the runway and take off'. They never flew with A-bombs over England.[17]

B–66 of the 47th Bomb Wing. (G. Wickstrum)

B–45 4551 at Sculthorpe. 84th Bomb Sqn May 1958. Scrapped in 1964. (G. Wickstrum)

Routine training would consist of dropping practice bombs called *Blue Beetles*, made of cement but similar in weight and aerodynamics to the real thing, over ranges like Jurby on the Isle of Man. At other times, they would fly to radar bomb scoring (RBS) sites all over the UK to simulate the bombing of factories or military sites. Châteauroux in France was a diversion airfield for a rendezvous with a KB-50 of the 420th Refuelling Squadron in case fuel was running low, or a possible alternative for landing in case fog closed in at Sculthorpe, which it frequently did. In addition, there was a monthly bombing competition between the squadrons, called Operation 'Gift', which kept the crews on their toes.

DEVELOPMENTS NATIONWIDE

Even as the Royal Air Force was developing its own fighter force with Gloster Javelins and Hawker Hunters, yet another American supersonic fighter had arrived at Bentwaters in August 1958: the McDonnell F-101 Voodoo. By the end of 1959 and the start of 1960 there was a formidable line-up of British and US air defence and nuclear strike capability, with the bombers of US Strategic Air Command, the tactical bomber wing at Sculthorpe, the RAF's V-bomber force building up its strength and now the Thor missile deployments. In the meantime, the Soviet Union was hardly idle, as was amply demonstrated by the display of hardware in the annual Moscow May Day military parades. Precise information about Soviet missile development was hard to come by, which was the reason for the deployment in East Anglia, and elsewhere, of the Boeing RB-47 Stratojet and the formidable Lockheed U-2 photoreconnaissance 'spy' aircraft. The U-2 was an odd-looking aircraft seen over Lakenheath as early as 1956, which soon proved its worth in high-altitude reconnaissance flights over the Soviet Union, taking over from where the RB-45s had left off. It was a U-2, previously based at Lakenheath and flown by Central Intelligence Agency (CIA) pilot Gary Powers from his base in Pakistan, which was shot down over the Soviet Union on 1 May 1960, causing a major international incident and the collapse of the Khrushchev–Eisenhower summit in Paris.[18]

The author recalls the sight of U-2s (now designated TR-1s) based at Sculthorpe in the 1980s as they practised circuits and landings near his home at Harpley, near Fakenham. Their lengthy tapered wings and strange whine marked them out as different from other jet aircraft from the base.

'LIVING WITH THE THING'

A dramatic article appeared in the *Sunday Graphic* of 11 September 1960 written by Derek Agnew headed 'Living with the Thing', describing life at Sculthorpe for the personnel of 'the biggest American base in Britain'. It showed a photograph of a B-66 of the 47th Bomb Wing, labelled 'In this belly 10 megatons of oblivion […] While the jets roar, airmen and wives shop with dimes and dollars'. In Main Street, Sculthorpe, it said, 'you can buy anything from a car to a haircut'. The timing of the article had coincided with the Trades Union Congress (TUC) Conference, which had split over the question of Britain's hydrogen bomb, so the issue of nuclear weapons was a very topical one.

The article continued:

> After a week of TALK about the H-bomb, take a close-up look at the families that sleep and eat and dance in its shadow […] I watched the airmen scramble for their sleek B-66 Destroyer bombers – not knowing whether or not they were on a mission that heralded the end of mankind […] and back in London I find it hard to realise that that the dedicated world I found at the end of a few hours' drive along the A11 really exists.

Agnew described the '2,000 British acres trodden for so long now by American feet' to see if the 'unspeakable horror in their midst shows on the faces and in the minds of those who exist behind barbed wire and machine-gun nests.'

He witnessed a few of the 1,000 children playing baseball, people shopping along the main street, two babies being born every 24 hours, five airmen getting married the previous week, 775 people attending church on Sunday and 1,000 pints of blood being donated to the Health Service – 'all against a background of warming-up jets', as the writer put it.

> We sit in the briefing room of the 47th Bombardment Wing in that part of the base where security means hard-eyed Air Police and passes and signs like 'Strictly Classified'. The Nissen hut must have looked just the same nearly two decades ago when the Englishmen who sat there hummed Glenn Miller tunes …Agnew talked to 32-year-old Captain Andrew Mitchell who 'helps himself from the ever-simmering coffee pot …':"No, we never think about it. It's a job, and none of us think for a moment, deep inside, that we'll ever have to finish it."

The journalist liked Captain Mitchell and his comrades and found them 'older, mature and domesticated rather than young tigers spoiling for a fight […] But when I looked at their strained faces I did not envy the £80 or so they earn a week.'

He described the face Sculthorpe shows the visitor:

> with its shopping parades, cinema, theatre, hospital, clubs, church, housing estate (complete with zebra crossings), golf course, go-kart track, gymnasium and every other facet of a modern community which appears to have not a care in

the world [...] BUT ARE THERE DOUBTS BEHIND ITS FACE AND A COLD HORROR WHERE ITS HEART SHOULD BE?

Not according to the chaplain, Father Normile, who said:

I probably know the secret fears of the men and women on this base more than anyone [...] the thought of being physically close to the Bomb doesn't worry them. They don't treat it lightly – but neither do they let the sheer horror of what it's all about weigh down on them.

The article concluded:

No one looks forward to the day when Sculthorpe goes under the plough again more hopefully than the Americans who live there. If and when that time comes they should haul a rusting harmless bomb to the top of a nearby hill and on it inscribe REST IN PEACE.[19]

NOTES

1. Bowyer, M.J.F., *Force for Freedom,* p.119.
2. Flightglobal Archive, 29 March 1957 pp.411–14.
3. *The Stars and Stripes,* 19 Feb. 1957.
4. *Sculthorpe's Weekly News Summary,* 17 May 1957.
5. Roger Lowe, interview with author, 10 Oct. 2011.
6. Bowyer pp.137–9.
7. *Eastern Daily Press,* 7 Dec. 1957.
8. Roger Lowe.
9. Bob Collis, information and photographs, March 2012.
10. *Eastern Daily Press,* 31 Oct. 1958
11. *Mother Jones* magazine, Nov./Dec. 1998.
12. *The Times,* 7 Dec. 1962.
13. *Daily Mirror,* 15 Dec. 1962.
14. *Eastern Daily Press,* 3 Nov. 1958.
15. Quoted in *Glory Days* by Wolfgang W.E. Samuel (Schiffer Military History 2008) pp.59–68. [See Bibliography].
16. Ibid. pp.62–5.
17. Ibid. p.63.
18. Bowyer, pp.150–1.
19. *Sunday Graphic,* 11 Sept. 1960.

14. DEACTIVATION TO STANDBY

'The 10-year dollar honeymoon is at an end.'

At the start of 1961 Sculthorpe continued to be a front-line nuclear base, with the B-66 Destroyers ready to counter any threat from the Soviet Union. The B-50s of the 420th Air Refuelling Squadron still performed a key role in supporting air operations. A fresh development was the ability to transfer fuel from the USAF tankers to the RAF V-bombers and vice versa, something that would greatly enhance Allied air co-operation in any war. This was demonstrated at Sculthorpe during Operation 'Flood Tide' early in the year, in which an RAF Valiant successfully refuelled a B-66, F-100 and F-101, with a Valiant and Javelin receiving fuel from a B-50.[1]

The New Year began with a new US President, John F. Kennedy, and there was already a hint of change to come when rumours spread of a restriction in the numbers of American dependants in overseas bases, to reduce the strain on the US budget. This came as a shock to UK landlords and estate agents, especially in East Anglia, although the decision was later rescinded.

The *Daily Express* ran an article by defence correspondent Chapman Pincher on 11 April 1961 under the heading 'Big US Air Base is to be Closed', outlining President Kennedy's economy drive and the plan to cut back Sculthorpe 'and two other bases' to satellite airfield status within a period of two years. The following day the same newspaper described the impact this would have on the local community under the heading 'They Wait for an Airfield to Die'. Publicans, hoteliers, landlords and landladies, shopkeepers and local businessmen all expressed their dismay and what this would mean to towns like Fakenham and Hunstanton. It would hit 2,000 civilian workers, according to the article, in an area where alternative employment prospects were bleak.

There was an immediate reaction, with questions in the House of Commons addressed to the prime minister. Norfolk County Council wrote to the Secretary of State for Air outlining concerns for the area if the rumours were true. The US Third Air Force offered no comment at this stage.

The facts were not slow in coming. On 22 June, both *The Times* and *New York Times* reported that the US Department of Defense had named three UK bases to be reduced in size or 'phased down', to use the term the Americans preferred: Sculthorpe (the biggest), Chelveston in Northamptonshire and Alconbury in Huntingdonshire, with complete closure planned for a fourth, Bruntingthorpe in Leicestershire.

The consequences for Sculthorpe were outlined by *The Times*. By June 1962 the base would have a USAF contingent comprising weather, communications and support staff only, with no flying units. Some 2,700 military personnel would be affected, along with 5,800 dependants and around 680 civilian employees. On top of that, the Americans would be leaving 'one of the best equipped sites in the country' with modern housing, new schools, a chapel, playing fields, a nine-hole golf course and a gymnasium recently built for £50,000. The surrounding towns and villages would suffer loss and the local district council would be poorer by £40,000 a year in rates. The one ray of hope was that new industry might move into the area, according to Mr R.I. Maxwell, the council planning officer.[2]

The running down of the four bases, the first closures of a proposed total of twenty-one establishments, was designed to save the US defence budget over £3 million a year (or over $9 million) in operating costs but it was made clear that this was part of a reorganisation and restructuring of USAF capability in Europe and not an attempt to reduce it. However, East–West tension during the summer of 1961, culminating in the building of the Berlin Wall in August, led to a rethink. Was the wrong message being conveyed to the Kremlin? Accordingly, in October, US Air Force Secretary Eugene Zuckert announced that the closures would be postponed indefinitely in the light of recent developments. But by now it was clear that it was a question of *when* and not *if* the axe was going to fall. Apart from the obvious economic savings involved, what was going on in the minds of American defence planners?

NEW TECHNOLOGIES AND NEW STRATEGIES

By the end of the 1950s, massive changes were taking place which would affect US Air Force deployments in Europe. At the strategic level, the newly elected President Charles de Gaulle of France gave notice in 1959 that US nuclear forces should vacate the country by the mid-1960s and that France would press ahead with its own nuclear deterrent. This would clearly affect NATO and the US Air Force in the UK and Germany, but it took time for the implications to be worked through.

As we have already seen, the 1960s ushered in the age of the intercontinental ballistic missile, foreshadowed by the launch of *Sputnik I* in October 1957, the world's first artificial satellite. The USSR's launch of their first ICBM in 1957 was followed by the launch of the Titan ICBM by the Americans in February 1959. The following June saw the arrival of the first US ballistic missile-carrying submarine, the USS *George*

Washington. The nuclear arms race was entering a new and more deadly phase. It seemed that tactical bombers like the B-66 were already becoming obsolete.

This was made even more apparent by the shooting down of the U-2 of Gary Powers during a spy mission over the USSR in May 1960 by Soviet surface-to-air missiles. This highlighted the vulnerability of conventional bombers in the face of Soviet defences. 'To survive, bombers had to change tactics – fly low instead of high and deliver their weapons using the preferred LABS [Low Altitude Bomb System] toss-bombing maneuver [*sic*], something the B-66 was not built to execute.'[3]

It was speculated that the B-66 would be replaced by the Republic F-105 Thunderchief, one of the new generation of supersonic fighter-bombers capable of delivering nuclear weapons. On 15 January 1960, Lakenheath had witnessed the arrival of the North American F-100 Super Sabres of the 48th Tactical Fighter Wing (TFW) – 'The Statue of Liberty Wing' – from Chaumont in France. The F-100 was the first operational combat aircraft to achieve supersonic speed in level flight. The 48th TFW was destined to have a close link with Sculthorpe in future years and continues today as the mainstay of the US Air Force in East Anglia.

B-66 MISSING

It was business as usual at the base. Operational routines continued, but tragedy struck on 26 October 1961 in what appears to have been the last B-66 loss of the 47th Bomb Wing at Sculthorpe, when an aircraft from the 85th Bomb Squadron

crashed in the North Sea off the Norfolk coast with the loss of all the crew: Major Paul Brooks, pilot, and Captains Paul J. Savage and Ralph Davenport. In a vain effort to rescue the crew, there was an extensive search by land and sea, including the Cromer and Wells lifeboats. By way of recognition of these efforts, a commemorative plaque was presented to the Wells Lifeboat crew by the 47th Bomb Wing.

Commemorative plaque at Wells Lifeboat Station, Oct. 1961. (Allen Frary)

THE 'LEMON AND BLIZARD AFFAIR' OR 'SCULTHORPE AFFAIR'

During 1961, allegations surfaced about certain overruns and underruns in accounting for works services at the base between 1956 and 1961. It was alleged that payments had been made to Messrs Lemon and Blizard, private quantity surveyors, involving some overpayment to contractors, which amounted to £9,125 out of a total value of works' contracts of some £670,000 during the period 1956–59. A board of inquiry 'into Alleged Works Irregularities at RAF Sculthorpe' was established in September 1961. There was even a suggestion that some USAF staff had raised fictitious orders. The Director of Public Prosecutions ruled out criminal fraud so it was left to the formal enquiry to determine what had gone wrong. In the end it was concluded that mistakes had been made due to a possible staff shortage which resulted in a failure to check estimates thoroughly, rather than a systematic attempt to defraud or manipulate figures.[4]

1962: END OF AN ERA

In spite of a suggestion of a reprieve, there was to be no retreat from the decision to phase down the base. On 24 March 1962 *The Times* reported that the 47th Bomb Wing at Sculthorpe would be standing down during the summer and the aerial refuelling squadron (the 420th) transferred to Mildenhall. The USAF would continue to use Sculthorpe for weather, communication and other support roles. The remaining B-66 units in place at Bruntingthorpe in Leicestershire and Chelveston in Northamptonshire would be reallocated to other parts of the command. Bruntingthorpe was to be returned to the RAF and Chelveston retained by the USAF on the same basis as Sculthorpe.

Armed Forces Day in May 1962 must have been especially poignant, as it marked the 47th Bomb Wing's last at Sculthorpe and also its tenth anniversary in Norfolk. On the same day, the *Sculthorpe Scanner*, the weekly newspaper of the 47th BW, published since October 1958, produced its final edition.

On 22 June, the 47th Bomb Wing, the last permanent bomber wing to be based at Sculthorpe, was officially deactivated and personnel transferred in due course to Laughlin Air Force Base in Texas. In the meantime, a number of aircraft were reassigned to the 42nd Tactical Reconnaissance Squadron of the 10th Tactical Reconnaissance Wing based at Chelveston and modified with an electronic countermeasures tail system. The 420th Air Refuelling Squadron remained at Sculthorpe for a further two years. The base was now placed under the command of the 7375th Combat Support Group.

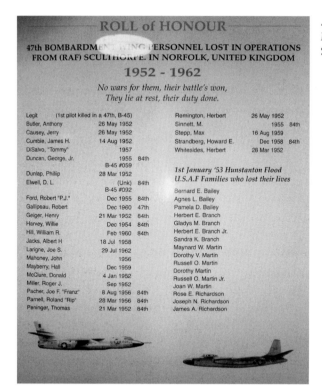

47th Bomb Wing Memorial, Green Park, Sculthorpe. (Author)

LOCAL SCENE

To local people the impending phase down of the base may not have been as dramatic or sudden as many had predicted, or so it seemed to Roger Lowe, a young Docking lad:

> We didn't know about the run down. We hardly knew they had gone. The families must have stopped coming probably about 1958 or 1959. They built the housing up then. They had a huge caravan park there. Gradually they must have been drawing people back into the base from outlying areas.

Verrall Grimes continued to work in the NCO Club as it still remained open as a transit centre for personnel on their return to the United States via Mildenhall.

Given the size of the base, it was a massive logistical task to organise the movement of so many personnel and their families with their possessions back to the United States, even on a phased basis. Inevitably there was some wastage, as Roger Lowe discovered in Docking:

> Over the road there was a barn owned by my father and rented to some Americans. It used to be an old blacksmith's workshop. A couple of guys did

their bits and pieces there. When there was one leaving we would hang around and they didn't take much stuff back with them because to them it was ten a penny and if you were lucky you could pick up some tools or an air gun. When they finally left the workshop they left no end of equipment – tools, vices – we still have one they left. A huge vice – it must have cost a fortune. My eldest brother sold a lot of the stuff off.

Simon Thorpe, a regular visitor to the base to play sport, recalled what he saw as some families prepared to leave in the early 1960s: 'The houses were emptied and the items were just taken outside and buried in a deep pit: tyres, fridges, cookers, cutlery. From the Motor Pool there were 45 gallon drums and electric motors. Some of the items were new and still sealed up.'

Between April and August 1962 it was estimated that the number of Sculthorpe personnel plus their dependants had declined from 8,500 to 2,500, and this was expected to have a considerable impact locally. Not so, according to an article in *The Times* of 14 August 1962 with the headline 'Americans Depart but Norfolk Slump Fails to Arrive'. It appeared that the death of the local economy had been greatly exaggerated, at least as far as many local people were concerned: 'Have they really gone?' was one comment quoted. Others predicted that the worst was yet to come. Looking at the facts, the picture was more complicated than previous doom and gloom forecasts had indicated.

The Times article estimated that at least half of the total of over 700 civilian employees no longer worked at the base, but of these many had retired, taken other jobs or, as government employees, had been transferred to alternative posts. The impact on local traders, shopkeepers, estate agents and landlords in the local towns and villages of the departure of the 1,300 American families living off the base was surprisingly slight, with a few exceptions. The Fakenham businessman Mr Val Aldiss had found little change in the turnover from his stores, and one estate agent in Fakenham claimed that turnover from his properties in 1962 had already exceeded that of the previous year. The article continued: 'Everyone knows a man who knows a man who has suffered. No one seems to have had the experience himself.'

The idea that letting to American families had been a property bonanza was shown to have been far off the mark, as base housing officers had kept close watch on local rent levels and vetoed them if they seemed excessive. Five pounds a week was quoted as the typical rent for a three-bedroomed bungalow, although officers might pay more. Some of the local pubs and hotels had seen a decline in their trade but Sculthorpe was not the only air force base in the wider community – there were RAF stations at West Raynham, Marham and Coltishall amongst others, although RAF Bircham Newton was due to close in December 1962.

One factor that might have mitigated the decline in trade was that in recent days Sculthorpe personnel had included a higher proportion of single men, and in any case it had been the practice for most Americans and their families to shop at the

AFEX (Air Force Exchange – Base Exchange or BX) rather than outside the base. The estimate was that 90 per cent of the spending was on the base, with 10 per cent in local shops.

Thus the picture was not entirely depressing, although there was a genuine fear that the base would close completely. There were other reasons for anxiety about the local economy, with the increasing mechanisation of farming, the biggest industry in Norfolk, causing job losses exceeding anything resulting from the closure or run down of Sculthorpe.[5]

The *New York Times* took up the story in an article of 23 August 1962 headed 'British Town [i.e. Fakenham] Thrives Despite Closing of US Base'. The prediction that cattle would soon be grazing on what was left of the base clearly had not happened, and one farmer commented: 'I tell you that Uncle Sam spends fewer dollars than is generally believed.' One exception seemed to be the owner of the Glebe Hotel in Hunstanton, the largest in the town, who claimed to have lost thousands of pounds since the Americans left.[6]

NEW CRISIS AND LIFE GOES ON

While the debate over Sculthorpe was being carried on, there was no lessening of international tension during the summer and autumn of 1962. If anything, the most dangerous crisis of the Cold War was yet to come – the Cuban missile crisis of October 1962, when the world was on the brink of nuclear war over the Soviet decision to site nuclear missiles on the island of Cuba. The fact that the 47th Bomb Wing was no longer at Sculthorpe made it no less of a target as a prime American base. On 22 October as the crisis developed, all US armed forces were placed on full alert and ordered from DEFCON (Defence Condition) five to DEFCON three, just two stages from war. The only other occasion of DEFCON three followed the terrorist attack on the Twin Towers in New York in September 2001. On 25 October, at the height of the crisis, the US military was ordered to DEFCON two, one stage before actual war.[7]

Sculthorpe was sidelined compared to the active RAF base of Marham and the Thor missile bases at Pickenham and Feltwell. The only flying units present were the 420th Air Refuelling Squadron and a detachment of the 28th Weather Squadron with its WB-50Ds. With the 47th Bomb Wing deactivated, there was no nuclear strike component any longer at the base. While the crisis lasted, the refuelling aircraft were on standby for the Woodbridge and Bentwaters units. By the end of October the emergency had passed.

The local community was grateful for American help during the freezing winter of 1962–63, when snow blocked the Sculthorpe runways and the local roads. Massive snow blowers were put to use to keep the base open and to enable locally based airmen to get into work. The knock-on effect was that surrounding roads were cleared in a fraction of the time it would have taken snow ploughs to do the job.

DEATH OF A PRESIDENT

There was worldwide shock at the assassination of President John F. Kennedy in Dallas on 22 November 1963, and there can be few people who fail to remember what they were doing on that tragic day. Not least among them was Airman Second Class John Northcut of the 7375th Combat Support Group based at Sculthorpe. That Friday evening he and his wife were settling down to an evening of listening to Radio Luxembourg when they caught the words: 'We extend our condolences to Mrs Kennedy.' Then the broadcast was resumed, a mix of popular music.

Not realising what had happened, John took the shuttle bus as usual to Sculthorpe and was shocked to hear the news and that the base had been placed on full alert the previous day. All airmen who lived off base had been recalled immediately and he had not reported in, causing him to fear a summons to the base commander's office for a reprimand and possibly even a jail sentence.

As it turned out he heard nothing more, except that there had been a breakdown in the normal channels of communication, by which certain airmen in a location were responsible for informing the others on a list they had. On this occasion the sergeant responsible was absent in London for the weekend and could not be reached by the base, with the result that John was not notified of the emergency. He summed up his thoughts on the incident: 'Since I had been born and raised in Dallas, it was an extremely embarrassing time for me, both on the base and in our village of Hunstanton. I was upset that such a thing could happen at all, and even more so in the city of my birth.'[8]

From Sculthorpe, John was eventually transferred to Laon Air Base in France. After leaving the Air Force, he worked first in private business and later with the United Nations.

AIR REFUELLERS LEAVE

Earlier in November 1963, in a further consolidation of the US Air Force presence, it was announced that two more bases were to be handed over to the RAF: Fairford in Gloucestershire and Greenham Common in Berkshire. Sculthorpe was finally to lose the 420th Air Refuelling Squadron in the following year; the last permanent flying unit to be stationed at the base. The KB-50Js were more than 15 years old and were too slow to match the speed of the latest tactical jets, so in March 1964 the last seven aircraft would leave for Edwards Air Force Base and the squadron deactivated.

CLOSURE AND FUTURE DEBATE

With the departure of the 420th ARS, the 7375th Combat Support Group, which had administered the base since 1962, was disbanded and the base was handed back to the Ministry of Defence (which had just absorbed the old Air Ministry). Sculthorpe became a standby base, mainly for general storage. The former Site No. 7 (from the RAF plan 1949) was sold and plans were in hand to sell much of the remainder of the domestic and technical sites. The base was to be closed except for the base housing, which was allocated as an overspill facility to personnel and their families from the Kestrel P1127 Evaluation Squadron (the forerunner of the Harrier) which had formed at RAF West Raynham in October 1964 and remained there until November 1965. Other West Raynham families from personnel of No. 41 Squadron, comprising the Bloodhound surface-to-air missile system, utilised accommodation at Sculthorpe from September 1965, in addition to families from RAF Marham.

By March 1964, the number of USAF personnel stationed at Sculthorpe had declined to 1,200 with around 1,754 dependants. There were 178 UK civilian employees, 176 Air Ministry employees and 104 from the Ministry of Public Buildings and Works. The actual closure date was scheduled for 1 July 1964.[9]

In what seemed like a last-ditch effort, the *Daily Express* ran an article with the headline 'Fight to Save Doomed Town', reporting that a telegram had been sent to Prime Minister Sir Alec Douglas-Home to seek a firm decision about the future of the base. Local authorities were concerned that delay might choke off any hope for new investment. The article summed up the facilities that were at risk: four hangars, factory space, 360 houses, a cinema and theatre, a golf course and the two finest buildings on the site – the gymnasium and chapel. 'It is a ready-made paradise for industrialists', said Mr Valentine Aldiss, chairman of the Chamber of Trade in Fakenham.[10]

Government policy about Sculthorpe at this stage was to have no policy, with the consequent neglect of the base except for the base housing. One of the possibilities mooted was development as a civil airport, but this was sidelined in favour of Stansted. Another was use by two Royal Artillery regiments, but Sculthorpe was considered second best compared to other establishments like North Weald near Epping and Horsham St Faith. It seemed a fairly depressing end to an illustrious past.

NOTES

1. Flightglobal Archive, 3 March 1961.
2. *The Times,* 22 June 1961.
3. Samuel, Wolfgang W.E., *Glory Days: The Untold Story of the Men who Flew the B-66* (Schiffer Military History 2008), p.70.
4. AIR 2/16134.

5. *The Times,* 14 Aug. 1962.
6. *New York Times,* 23 Aug. 1962.
7. Wilson, Jim, *Britain on the Brink* (Pen & Sword 2012), p.8.
8. Northcut, John, email to author, 30 Dec. 2012.
9. AIR 2/16052, 'RAF Sculthorpe: USAF withdrawal and closure 1961–66.'
10. Ibid., *Daily Express* cutting, April 1964.

15. STANDBY TO STANTA

1966–72

It did not take long for Sculthorpe to decline into a state of dilapidation, with runways unused and overgrown, buildings empty and neglected. The base housing was useful as 'overspill' accommodation for families from RAF West Raynham, and the surroundings were a paradise for adventurous children as a gigantic play area all to themselves. However, it was not long before there was going to be yet another change in the status of the base.

In early 1966, President de Gaulle gave notice that American forces should leave France and that France would withdraw from NATO by 1967. This meant that new force requirements in the UK led to Sculthorpe being reopened, first as a storage depot in early 1967 and then with Standby Dispersal Base status, essentially as a support base for the 48th Tactical Fighter Wing (TFW) based at Lakenheath and administered by the 7519th Combat Support Squadron (CSS). At first it was envisaged that only about 200 servicemen would be stationed at the base, with about forty civilians.

According to an official report of September 1967, there was a vast amount of work to be completed before the base could be returned to operational status. The surveyor remarked that he had 'rarely spent a more depressing day than the one last week when I went over to the Station'. There was destruction resulting from the departure of the Americans when the base had been cannibalised for anything of use. Local thieves and looters had run riot and children from the married quarters had pillaged buildings and smashed windows, to a point that some considered the site beyond repair. The report continued: 'I am told that representations to the RAF parent station [West Raynham] and to parents of the children have been coldly received. Nobody seems to care that the taxpayers, here or in the States, will have to make good this wanton damage.'[1]

When the renovation work got under way, approximately two-thirds of the buildings were demolished and there was refurbishment of many existing buildings. Some new buildings were added. Much of the work was directed from Washington DC, and Barry Wells, former Property Services Agency (PSA) employee, maintained that the defence chiefs in Washington had inadequate maps and were instructing staff on site to refurbish Nissen huts and demolish some of the permanent buildings. Surplus roofs and timberwork were removed and the Amey Roadstone Construction Company crushed up the remaining concrete, much of which was taken away and used in the building of new roads around Peterborough. Much the same process was happening at North Creake airfield.

With the refurbishment of the base came new possibilities such as making available the resurfaced runways for flight-testing the first British prototype of Concorde. This was proposed in the summer of 1968 for Sculthorpe and Elvington in Yorkshire, although as far as is known nothing came of the plan.[2]

1972–92

From 1972 to 1992, Sculthorpe continued to be a Standby Dispersal Base. The 7519th Combat Support Squadron continued to administer the base until early 1976. Dan Daley was a communication electronics technician in Detachment 3 of the 1979th Communications Squadron based at Sculthorpe from 1970 until 1975 and recalled that he was one of about 175 personnel on the base. He was a fourth generation Californian but spent the first five years of his married life with his wife Jan at the base housing in Sculthorpe. Their first two children were born at Lakenheath hospital.

Sign at the entrance to the base in 1975. Detachment 3 reported directly to the Comm. Squadron at RAF Lakenheath. (Dan and Jan Daley)

The new communications centre built in 1971-72. This was new 'cutting-edge, high speed' telecommunications equipment that replaced the old teletype equipment. (Dan and Jan Daley)

With the disbandment of the 7519th CSS in 1976 the airfield was handed over to the Ministry of Defence, becoming Detachment 1 of the 48th Tactical Fighter Wing (TFW). There was a small US presence throughout, and from 1972 the base saw some annual exercises starting with *Flintlock V*, a combined US Army and USAF deployment exercise.

In support of the exercise, a Lockheed C-5 Galaxy airlift aircraft landed at Sculthorpe on 3 September 1972, the first aircraft to land there since 1964.[3] There was provision for up to six airlift aircraft types at the base during the exercise, including the Galaxy and the C-130 Hercules. It was decided to alternate future *Flintlock* exercises with the other Standby Deployment Base at Greenham Common, partly to ensure that both stations were kept up to the mark for future operational needs.

Visiting units often included the US Air National Guard for two weeks at a time, with A7 Vought Corsairs or F-4 Phantoms. Barry Wells claimed that the National Guard produced better pilots than the regular air force. They were often airline pilots doing weekend duties with the National Guard and hence very skilled and experienced. Roger Lowe recalled that they sometimes held open days at the base, allowing visitors to sit in the cockpits of the aircraft. The base also hosted RAF *Bolthole* exercises – the term used for the airfield employment when runways elsewhere were being resurfaced or refurbished, as happened later at Marham or Coltishall (see Appendix V).

TACAN (Tactical Air Navigation System) with the ground-based radio site on the flight line in 1975. These were kept in good working order in case they were needed by aircraft diverted to Sculthorpe. (Dan and Jan Daley)

Vought A7 Corsairs of the Ohio Air National Guard, on various deployments during the 1980s. (Richard Jermy)

A fresh role allocated for the base in 1981 was a Mutual/Military Assistance Program (MAP) by which surplus aircraft from the Danish and Norwegian air forces were flown in for conversion to the Turkish Air Force. Aircraft types involved included North American F-100s, Lockheed Starfighters and T-33s. Other aircraft arrived for scrapping from the French Air Force, including Mystère IVs. A handful of aviation museums like the Norfolk and Suffolk Aviation Museum at Flixton received permission to obtain a few of the aircraft for conservation as long as they undertook the task of dismantling and transport.[4]

In late 1984, Sculthorpe became one of sixteen military bases targeted for demonstrations by the Campaign for Nuclear Disarmament (CND) in the 'Snowball' campaign, protesting at the stationing of cruise missiles at Greenham Common. Symbolic wire cutting of the perimeter fencing took place, followed by a number of arrests for criminal damage, including the General Secretary of CND, Monsignor Bruce Kent.

Plans were drawn up for hardened aircraft shelters (HAS) during the 1980s, but these were shelved later as the Cold War ended. In October 1992, the US Air Force finally hauled down the 'Stars and Stripes' for the last time at Sculthorpe. Job losses due to the closure involved thirty-eight local civilians, with twenty-five Ministry of Defence policemen and thirty American servicemen being posted to other units. The site was then handed over to the Ministry of Defence.

TR-1s seen at Sculthorpe at various times during the 1980s. The aircraft could be inspected on open days but looking into the cockpit was forbidden. (Richard Jermy)

TUESDAY Lynn News, 6 October, 1992 7

W Norfolk air force era comes to an end

FRIDAY marked the end of an air force era when the 'Stars and Stripes' were lowered from their flagpole at RAF Sculthorpe from where they have flown for more than 30 years.

The departure of the United States Air Force from the base near Fakenham was marked by an official military ceremony. But local civilians, some who could remember arrival of the USAF in the 1950s, joined in the farewell.

RAF Sculthorpe was the largest American airfield in the UK with more than 10,000 people including servicemen and their families attached.

The last 38 industrial employees were made redundant last week, confirmed an MoD spokesman, and 25 MoD policemen have been posted to other bases throughout the country. "Initially the USAF was due to

close down the base in October 1995, but with the end of the Cold War and the American withdrawals from Europe everything gathered momentum," said the spokesman.

"Sculthorpe is now like many bases in England which have an undecided future. There are a lot of Army colleagues returning from Europe but we still don't know how the bases will be used."

He confirmed the buildings will remain empty but kept secure.

A spokesman from USAF Lakenheath, confirmed the keys of the base had been handed over to the MoD and USAF personnel had left.

● Bugler David Hollingsworth plays at the lowering of the United States flag. (92/10/20)

PICTURES: ALAN MILLER

● Station commander Major Joe Kimbrell and his wife, Debra, cut the cake to mark the end of an American era at RAF Sculthorpe. Staff Sgt Bret Wanty (left) and Senior Airman Todd Cook hold the cake. (92/10/21)

'Stars and Stripes' lowered for the last time, Friday 2 October 1992. (*Lynn News*)

Boeing Chinook at work during a STANTA exercise. (Richard Jermy)

1992 TO PRESENT

Since October 1992, the main airfield site has been a Ministry of Defence (MOD) training area operated by the Stanford Battle Area (STANTA), which means access is restricted except to local farming activities. A further phase of demolition work took place during February and March 2012 within the MOD perimeter on a total of some forty structures, which included some storage buildings and redundant electricity and water supply structures. The 1945-era control tower remains intact along with most of the buildings in the former bomb/munitions storage area.

NOTES

1.   AIR 2/18131, 1967–72 Air Ministry and Ministry of Defence: Regional Director, Eastern Region, 14/9/67.
2.   AIR 2/18131, 1967–72: extracts on Concorde flight-testing.
3.   Baldwin, J., RAF Sculthorpe: *50 Years of Watching and Waiting* (1999), p.25.
4.   Ibid. pp.30–1.

16. AIRFIELD INFRASTRUCTURE

Grid Reference: TF 860315
Parishes: Sculthorpe, Dunton, Tattersett.
Nearest town: Fakenham, 4 miles to east.

1946 aerial photograph. (Norfolk Historic Environment Record, Norfolk County Council)

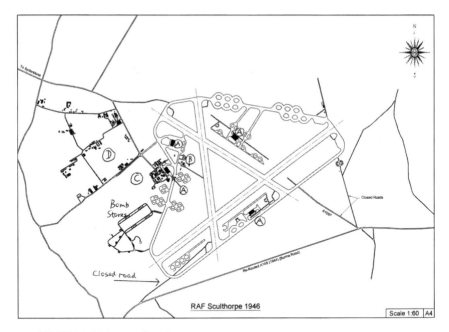

1946 AIRFIELD PLAN: LEGEND
Note closed roads and re-routed A148 (The 'Burma Road').
A. Hangars.   B. Watch Office/Control Tower.   C. Technical site.   D. Domestic site.

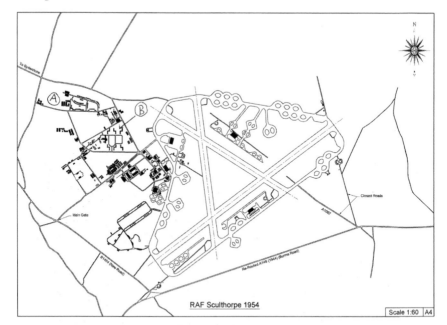

1954 AIRFIELD PLAN: LEGEND
Note development in Domestic and Technical sites. Main changes since 1946: construction of RAF married accommodation at A and completion of 'Z' blocks at B. In mid to late 1950s the new B1454 was completed to improve link on the western side of the airfield and to replace the closed section of the A1067.
A. RAF housing.   B. 'Z' blocks.

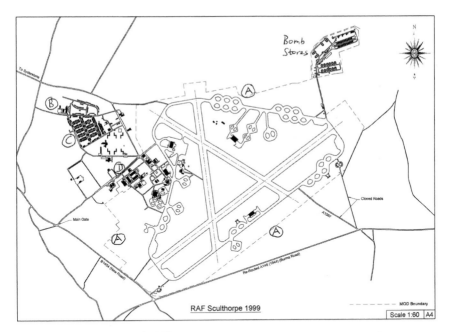

1999 AIRFIELD PLAN: LEGEND

In 1999 much of the original airfield infrastructure remained intact. Note that the Bomb Stores had been relocated in the later 1950s and were now within the MOD perimeter.

A. MOD perimeter fence enclosing STANTA training area.

B. Blenheim Park village (former RAF housing).

C. Wicken Green village (former 'Tobacco' or 'Commodity' housing built for the USAF).

D. Tattersett Business Park (formerly part of the Technical site).

(1946, 1954 and 1999 plans drawn by Chris Lowe).

Approach to Sculthorpe from Fakenham, c. 1956, heading north-west. (David Whitaker)

1942–49: MAIN PHASES OF DEVELOPMENT

1942: airfield construction began.

January 1943: airfield opened as satellite for RAF West Raynham.

May 1943: first flying units arrived. Station became independent, no longer a satellite.

May 1944: flying units left. Station placed on care and maintenance basis. Upgrading to Very Heavy Bomber (VHB) station began.

Station effectively closed until December 1948, although in occasional use by RAF. Station reopened December 1948.

February 1949: first US Air Force units arrived.

1951–63: THE US AIR FORCE AT SCULTHORPE

Summary of airfield facilities in November 1956

[Source: AIR 2/10717 Works Services, RAF Sculthorpe Works Commission Inquiry, 7 November 1956]

(a) Runways:

No. 1 Runway, bearing 053°–233°, length 8,955ft, width 300ft, overruns 600ft NE, 1,000ft SW. Comment: could be developed to 10,000ft with 1,000ft overruns.

No. 2 Runway, bearing 121°–301°, length 6,060ft, width 300ft, overruns 600ft NW, 600ft SE. The approach was said to be fouled by a barn. Development possibilities – nil.

No. 3 Runway, bearing 172°–352°, length 6,000ft, width 300ft, overruns 600ft to N, 660ft to S. Development possibilities – in theory runway could be extended by 1,000ft to S but this would interfere with the already diverted A148 highway.

(b) Hangars:

Four T2 Hangars, Nos. 24, 78, 94 and 120.

Demolished around 2008.

Also eight E6 (small blister type hangars), of which one remains (on eastern side of airfield).

(c) Domestic accommodation:

This allowed for accommodation for 260 officers and 3,000 enlisted men.

(d) Bomb stores:

New bomb stores were being constructed on the NE side of the airfield.

Between 1956 and 1958 the bomb dump on the SW side of the airfield was closed.

(e) Roads:

Just as the 'Burma Road' (A148) from Fakenham to Tattersett had been completed to the south of the airfield (see Chapter Three) during the mid-1950s, there was a further proposal to realign the Tattersett–Syderstone road to the south-west of the airfield to replace the closed portion of the A1067, and thereby improve the access from Fakenham to the western (main) gate of the airfield. This road (the present B1454) was to bypass Tattersett and Syderstone and improve the link to Bircham Newton and Docking. However, it was not without some controversy as it involved objections from Syderstone Parish Council to the proposed route cutting through Syderstone Common and therefore violating common rights dating back to the sixteenth century. The objections were overruled in an enquiry and the road building went ahead in the later 1950s. One result was that by 1958 the bomb stores were moved to the north-east side of the airfield as they would have been in too close proximity to the new public highway and raise possible security risks.

New road (B1454) being constructed in late 1950s. Scene outside Highfield House in Syderstone Common during construction. (Mrs Odell)

New road during construction in area of Highfield House. (Mrs Odell)

Road shortly after completion, later 1950s. (Mrs Odell)

Same stretch of road, 2013. (Author)

(f) Underground fuel pipelines:

Fuel was supplied to the base via an underground pipeline from the 1940s until around 1968. Government Pipelines and Storage Systems (GPSS) operated the route in a countrywide network via Thetford (USAF bases at Mildenhall and Lakenheath) with a branch off to Shouldham for RAF Marham and thence to a small depot at Harpley Dams near Massingham. For the final 5 miles to Sculthorpe airfield via Tattersett the pipeline ran parallel to and just north of the A148. At intervals where hedges were crossed, there are small markers above ground to indicate the position of the pipeline. Near Castle Acre, just off Peddars Way, there was a small boosting station.

On the airfield, the fuel was then pumped to fuel dispensers situated at various points on the airfield as close as possible to the hardstandings where aircraft were parked. Some of the fuel dispensers are still visible on the south-east side of the airfield close to the A148.

The original pipeline was replaced during the 1970s and, although now disused, it remains *in situ* as do the rights of it to be used and maintained.

FORMER DOMESTIC AND TECHNICAL SITES

a) The former American married quarters and housing area is now a community comprising two 'villages' known as Blenheim Park and Wicken Green. The former RAF houses were built in 1948 of standard red brick in an area now called Blenheim Park and totalled 116. They were sold for private occupation during the 1990s. Immediately to the south of that are the Wicken Green prefabricated bungalows built by Wimpey in 1956–58, known as 'Commodity' or 'Tobacco houses', constructed in exchange for American tobacco. By the 1960s, there were a total of 210 commodity houses. The Wicken Green housing estate roadways are all marked as private. The various street names are redolent of their aviation past, including Halifax Crescent, Wellington Crescent, Stirling Road and Lancaster Road.
b) The domestic and technical sites are now an industrial area known as Tattersett Business Park which is accessible to the general public and for business. Street names such as Florida Boulevard, Georgia Road, Texas Avenue and Flag Road recall the American and military connection with the site.

Blenheim Park, 2013. (Author)

Technical and domestic site, *c.* 1956, looking towards north-west. Z Blocks and Base housing to right of picture. (David Whitaker)

SITE HISTORY TO PRESENT DAY: DOMESTIC AND TECHNICAL SITES

Based on 1976 Central Survey of Sculthorpe by Property Services Agency.

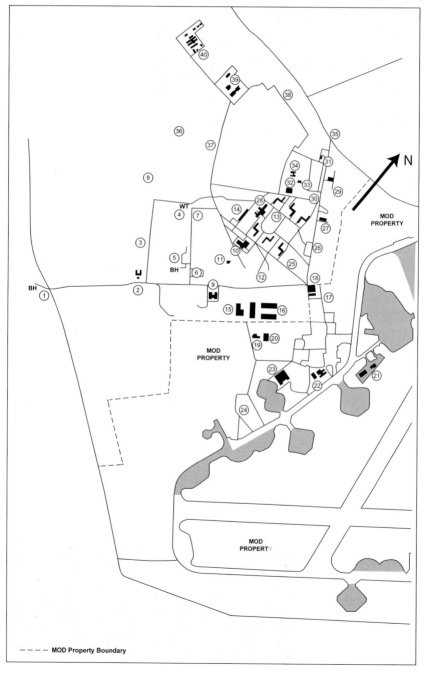

Borehole, July 2013.
(Author)

LEGEND

1. Borehole Bldg (BH) opposite entrance to camp (now Tattersett Business Park).

2. Former Gate No. 1. Now entrance to Tattersett Business Park.
Property Services Agency (PSA) Bldg. Began as Air Ministry, then Ministry of Works, Dept. of the Environment, and finally PSA.
[Site No. 3, Communal Site No. 2 (1949)]

3. Bldgs 519–520 (old nos.) Marston sheds – warehouses. Now demolished.
(to right, concrete Army Road gone but trees still there).
[Site No. 3, Communal Site No. 2 (1949)]

4. Water Tower (WT), demolished – now mobile phone masts. No. 1 Borehole water pumped to this for storage and then pumped to No. 47 hospital site.

PSA Building, c. 1980s.
(Richard Jermy)

Former RAF HQ, later
USAF Wing HQ, *c.* 1980s.
(Richard Jermy).

Wing HQ, partly demolished,
Sept. 2012. (Author)

5. Airmen's Club (now demolished). Next to Peach Tree Street (also demolished).

6. Officers' Club (both RAF and USAF) with car park. Now demolished. Squash courts. Note BH (borehole).
[Site No. 3, Communal Site No. 2 (1949)]

7. Police – USAF to 1963. MOD after 1963.
[Site No. 8 USAF (1949)]

8. Site of old Mess Hall (RAF and USAF). Now demolished.

9. Original RAF HQ Bldg, and later USAF (Wing HQ in 1955) – now being demolished. Bldg below that, Arts and Crafts Centre and out-of-hours club (part of HQ complex). Disposed of in 1963 and handed back to Air Ministry. Part of the site formerly Langham Glass.

10. Gymnasium – built approx. 1959. One of the few permanent buildings on site that is a permanent structure (now industrial use).

New Barrack block (Truman Hall) looking pristine in 1973. (Dan and Jan Daley)

Former USAF HQ, now within MOD perimeter, 2013. (Author)

HQ Building sign still visible. (Author)

Gateway between technical site and airfield. Taken in 1980s. (Richard Jermy)

11. Bldg south of gym – former boiler house (now Rudd Joinery).

12. Quonset huts site – now demolished (cleared by 1968).
[Site No. 4, Communal Quarters, WAAF Site No. 1 (1949)]

13. Z dorms. Single Airmen's Quarters. Originally RAF barrack blocks built c. 1948. Montgomery stated that every man should have his own room. But the USAF squeezed two men into each room in bunk beds.
[Adjacent to Site No. 8 (1949)]

14. New barrack block. (Truman Hall). Built around 1958-early 1960s.

15. Motor pool (USAF). Butler sheds. One bldg motor pool, the other for storage. (late-1950s bldgs).

16. Two Butler sheds – warehouses. Both bldgs late 1950s.

Control Tower, 'The pulse of the field'. (1953 Pictorial)

Control Tower in 1974 during the period of the 7519th Combat Support Squadron. (Dan and Jan Daley)

Control Tower in 1975. (Dan and Jan Daley)

Control Tower interior in 1975. (Dan and Jan Daley)

Note: Bldgs 17, 19–24 are now within the MOD restricted zone.

17. USAF HQ Bldg. Now within MOD restricted area.
MOD Police. (Had been USAF Police before 1963).
Former Parachute and Dinghy Bldg – up to 1963. Just to the south USAF HQ Bldg.

18. Adjacent to roundabout (former flagpole site) gateway to airfield adjoining storage bldg. This was the main link between the base and the airfield. Hangar 78 was towards the right into the airfield (now demolished).

Looking towards one of the Z blocks and the Medical Aid Station in 1973. (Dan and Jan Daley)

Medical Aid Station still looking pristine in the 1980s. (Richard Jermy).

Same view as top but with Medical Station demolished. (Author, July 2013)

19. New parachute and dinghy section.

20. Commissary store.

21. Old control tower and new control tower. Fire Section adjoining. Now within MOD restricted area. New control tower designed as for very heavy bomber station, opened in December 1948. The structure is three storeys high with a single storey annex leading off from side elevation, which houses the fire station and other services. The control tower is intact but now largely boarded up. To north and above, demolished Hangar 78 (T2 – taken down in 2008). Hangar 78 was the only one used until demolition.

22. USAF Operations Room.

23. Electronics building.

BX and Commissary 1980. (Richard Jermy)

BX and Commissary buildings in 2013. (Author)

Gas Station 1980. (Richard Jermy).

24. POL (Petroleum, Oil and Lubricants bldgs). To process JP4 jet fuel. Never used.

25. Station sick quarters and Medical Section (Medical Aid Stn), base dispensary. Now demolished.

26. USAF quarters. Now demolished.
[Site No. 6, WAAF Site No. 2 (1949)]

27. New American chapel, interdenominational, built around 1960. (Now industrial use).

28. Original RAF NAAFI. USAF took over NAAFI building. This complex once housed the NCO Club. Complex included reception centre, dining hall and children's playgroup.

Maj. Wood, Capt. Adams, Chaplains   Chaplains and base chapel. (1953 Pictorial)

Base chapel. (1955 Handbook)

Former chapel, now derelict, 2013. (Author)

Green Park Centre, 2013. (Author)

29. Base Exchange (BX/PX) and commissary. Present standing buildings dates from mid-1950s. Just below BX site of barber shop (Airmen). This site was the shopping centre – now demolished.

30. Opposite BX along road to generator shed, site of bowling alley.

Green Park Centre with memorials to 47th Bomb Wing, 2013. (Author)

Former American school, 2013. (Author)

31. Gas station.

32. Green Park Bldg (present day), formerly American All-Ranks Club (Butler bldg), and for a short time NCO Club. Started as American Youth Association (AYA) Bldg. To its left the old chapel (Nissen hut), formerly RAF and then used by the USAF until a new American chapel was built around 1960. The old chapel became a cinema.

33. Bldg near Green Park Base standby generator shed. Small bldg opposite that labelled 'Pete's Plaice and Take-Away', the former whisky and liquor store.

34. American school, now derelict. Built towards the end of the 1960s. The original school opposite was Nissen huts. The older children were bussed to Lakenheath as this was purely for primary age children. Area just to north housed a complex of structures (now demolished).

35. Former Gate No. 2. Now barred entry.

36. Bachelor officers' quarters. Now demolished.
[Site No. 7, USAF (1949)] – Site sold after 1963.

37. Tobacco (Commodity) housing – USAF married quarters. Now private housing as Wicken Green village.

38. Former RAF and later USAF married quarters, now private housing. Blenheim Park village.

No. 47 Tac Hospital, 1953.
(1953 Pictorial)

Hospital site, 1980s. Now demolished. (Richard Jermy)

T2 Hangar, c. 1980s.
Demolished c. 2008.
(Richard Jermy)

39. New school. Secondary. Built by the early 1960s. In current use.

40. No. 47 TAC hospital. Closed 1963 and now demolished. Also served as a church for a time. Also water tower. All the former buildings demolished.
[Site No. 5 Sick Quarters (1949)]
Former caravan site opposite.

General:
Hangars Nos. 24, 78, 94 and 120 (on southern side of airfield) – T2 type. All taken down in 2008.

OFF-BASE SITES (NOT ON MAP)

1. DECOY SITE:
Coxford Heath (Q/K site), TF 828 307
Operational during the Second World War.

2. RADIO BEACON SITES: operational 1950s until end 1960s.
Great Massingham Airfield (no details).
Walsingham, near Houghton St Giles, TF 918 356. Now demolished.
Coxford Heath, TF 823314. 3 sites (receiver, transmitter and transformer).
Now demolished.

3. SUBSTATIONS FOR APPROACH LIGHTING.
West Barsham, TF 898335. Standing structure.
Dunton, TF 881304. Standing structure.
East Rudham (location not known, now demolished).

4. THE SHOOTING BOX (LODGE):
South Creake MR TF 854 374.
Formerly the old shooting lodge of Earl Spencer, patron of South Creake. A Land Army hostel in 1939–40 and from 1944 used by the USAAF and later the USAF as a command and communications centre. Building demolished in 1960. Norfolk Heritage Explorer (NHER) number 42753.

5. LANGHAM USAF emergency hospital site. Used as an off-base storage site for the 47th BW at Sculthorpe. Location not known.

APPENDIX I

SOURCES AND BIBLIOGRAPHY

NATIONAL ARCHIVES, KEW

ARCHIVE SOURCES CONSULTED

1. AIR 27 – RAF FORM 540, SQUADRON OPERATIONAL RECORDS

AIR 27/1739, No. 342 (Lorraine) Sqn FFAF, 15 May to 19 July 1943.
AIR 27/1935, No. 487 (RNZAF) Sqn, 20 July to 31 Dec. 1943.
AIR 27/1924, No. 464 (RAAF) Sqn, 20 July to 31 Dec. 1943.
AIR 27/264, No. 21 Sqn (RAF), 27 Sept. to 31 Dec. 1943.
AIR 27/1323, No. 214 Sqn RAF, 16 Jan. to 16 May 1944.

2. AIR 28 – RAF FORM 540, STATION OPERATIONAL RECORDS – SCULTHORPE

AIR 28/692, 1943–44.
AIR 28/1110, 1949–51.

3. AIR 2 – AIR MINISTRY AND MINISTRY OF DEFENCE

AIR 2/10717, Airfield Works, Sculthorpe 1950–57.
AIR 2/10718, Airfield Works, Sculthorpe 1957–60.
AIR 2/16052, USAF withdrawal and closure 1961–66.
AIR 2/16134, Board of Inquiry, Works Irregularities 1961–63.
AIR 2/18131, RAF Sculthorpe Organisation 1967–72.
AIR 2/16109, RAF Sculthorpe, USAF Chapel.
AIR 2/18453, RAF Sculthorpe Organisation 1968–72.

4. CAB 129/57, Married Quarters for US Forces, 1952. (Online)

5. T 180/89 MINISTRY OF TRANSPORT

31 Aug. 1956. Plan.

NEWSPAPER SOURCES

The following newspaper archives were consulted at the British Library Newspapers at Colindale, Cambridge University Library, Norfolk Heritage Centre, Norfolk Millennium Library, Norwich, King's Lynn Library, *Eastern Daily Press* Library (Archant), Norwich.

The Times online.
Eastern Daily Press.
Daily Express.
Daily Mail.
Daily Mirror.
Daily Telegraph.
New York Times.
Lynn News and Advertiser.
The Star (Sheffield Newspapers Ltd).

GENERAL BIBLIOGRAPHY

General Works

Anderson, Bruce (editor), *Ploughshares and Propellers* (RAF Museum).
Andrew, Christopher, *The Defence of the Realm: The Authorized History of MI5* (Allen Lane, 2009).
Baldwin, Jim (ed.), *40 Years of RAF Sculthorpe 1943–1983* (Jim Baldwin Publishing, 1986).
—, *RAF Sculthorpe: 50 Years of Watching & Waiting* (Jim Baldwin, 1999).
Bowyer, Michael J.F., *2 Group RAF: A Complete History 1936–1945* (Faber, 1974).
—, *Action Stations Revisited, No. 1 Eastern England* (Crécy Publishing Limited, 2010).
—, *Force for Freedom: The USAF in the UK since 1948* (Patrick Stephens Limited, 1994).
Boyne, Walter J., *Beyond the Wild Blue: History of the US Air Force* (St Martin's Press, 1998).
Campbell, Duncan, *The Unsinkable Aircraft Carrier: American Military Power in Britain* (Paladin, 1986).
Delve, Ken, *The Military Airfields of Britain: East Anglia (Norfolk and Suffolk)* (Crowood Press Ltd, 2005).
English Heritage (Wayne D. Cockcroft et al.), *Cold War* (2003).
Eyton-Jones, Arthur, *Day Bomber* (Sutton Publishing Limited, 1998).
Francis, Paul, *British Military Airfield Architecture* (Patrick Stephens Limited, 1996).
Fredriksen, John C., *The B-45 Tornado: An Operational History* (McFarland & Company Inc., 2009).

Gunn, Peter B., *Flying Lives with a Norfolk Theme* (Peter B. Gunn, 2010).

Hall, R. Cargill, and Laurie, Clayton D., *Early Cold War Overflights 1950–56*: Symposium Proceedings: Vols 1–2 (Washington DC: Office of the Historian, National Reconnaissance Office, 2003).

Henry, Mike, DFC, *Air Gunner* (Goodhall, Crécy Publishing Limited, 1997).

Jackson, Robert, *Strike Force: the USAF in Britain since 1948* (Robson Books Ltd, 1986).

Lashmar, Paul, *Spy Flights of the Cold War* (Sutton Publishing Limited, 1996).

Lloyd, Alwyn T., *A Cold War Legacy: Tribute to SAC 1946–92* (Pictorial Histories Publishing Company Inc., 2000).

Samuel, Col. Wolfgang W.E., *I Always Wanted To Fly – America's Cold War Airmen* (University Press of Mississippi, 2001).

—, *Coming to Colorado: A Young Immigrant's Journey to become an American Flyer* (University Press of Mississippi, 2006).

—, *Glory Days: The Untold Story of the Men who Flew the B-66 Destroyer into the Face of Fear* (Schiffer Military History, 2008).

Streetly, Martin, *Confound and Destroy: 100 Group and the Bomber Support Campaign* (Jane's, 1985).

Wilson, Jim, *Britain on the Brink: The Cold War's Most Dangerous Weekend 27–28 October 1962* (Pen & Sword, 2012).

Windeler, Gary, *The Book of Sculthorpe* (Halsgrove, 2003).

Year Books

Sculthorpe, 1952: 84th Squadron, Light (Jet).
1953 Pictorial: Sculthorpe RAF Station England (47th Bomb Wing, Light).
47th Bomb Wing, England 1955.
1957 in England: Royal Air Force Station Sculthorpe Souvenir book.

Articles

Airfield Review (Journal of the Airfield Research Group), No. 135, Summer 2012.

Crampton, Squadron Leader J., 'RB-45C Operations' (Air Intelligence Symposium, Bracknell, Paper No. 7, Royal Air Force Historical Society).

Daily Telegraph, 7 February 1994: 'The night the RAF "bombed" Russia'.

Jackson, Robert, 'Strategic Air Power Post-War', (Air Intelligence Symposium).

Lashmar, Paul, 'Shootdowns', *Aeroplane Monthly*, August 1994.

Young, Prof. Ken, 'US "atomic capability" and the British forward bases in the early Cold War', *Journal of Contemporary History* 42(1), January 2007.

Online

www.47thbombwing.org (47th Bomber Wing Guest Book)

www.accident-report.com (USAF accidents from 1949–57)

www.afhra.af.mil (US Air Force Historical Research Agency)

www.aviastar.org (Virtual Aircraft Museum)

www.flightglobal.com (*Flight* magazine archive)

www.forcesreunited.org.uk

www.francisfrith.com (nostalgic photos/memories)

www.heritage.norfolk.gov.uk (Norfolk Heritage Explorer)

www.linewatch.co.uk (underground pipeline networks)

www.millionmonkeytheater.com/ForgottenJets

www.norfolk-airfields.co.uk

www.peakdistrictaircrashes.co.uk (aircraft accidents in Peak District)

www.PPRuNe.org (Professional Pilots Rumour Network)

www.pyramidiers.com (98th Bomb Group)

www.raf.mod.uk

www.sculthorpe.org (Sculthorpe airfield alumni)

www.spyflight.co.uk

www.strategic-air-command.com

www.usafnukes.com (Nuclear Weapons Technicians Association)

www.i-f-s.nl (The International F-104 Society)

www.wikipedia.org (aviation accidents and incidents)

APPENDIX II

SCULTHORPE COMMANDING OFFICERS

	From	To
Gp Capt. P.C. Pickard	30 July 1943	31 Dec 1943
Gp Capt. T.C. Dickens	1944	Airfield closure
		16 May 1944
Gp Capt. H.C. Parker	Jan. 1949	23 Jan. 1951
Wg Cdr W.L. Jones DFC	23 Jan. 1951	

After USAF units arrived the senior unit commander became the base commander.

APPENDIX III

UNITS 1943–44

Unit	Command	From
2 Heavy Glider Maintenance Unit 11 Heavy Glider Maintenance Section	2 Group RAF	10 February 1943
No. 342 Free French 'Groupe Lorraine' Sqn (Code OA)	2 Group RAF	W. Raynham 15 May 1943
No. 487 Sqn RNZAF (Code EG)	2 Group RAF	Methwold 20 July 1943
No. 464 Sqn RAAF (Code SB)	2 Group RAF	Methwold 21 July 1943
No. 21 Sqn (Code YH)	2 Group RAF	Hartford Bridge 27 September 1943
No. 214 Sqn (Code BU)	from 3 Group RAF to 100	Downham Mkt 16 January 1944
803rd Bomb Sqn (Provisional) USAAF	USAAF Eighth Air Force, (Det. 100 Group RAF)	January 1944
No. 1699 (Fortress Training) Flt (Code 4Z)	100 Group RAF	Formed 24 April 1944

To	Commanding Officer	Aircraft
15 March 1944	Horsa	
Gt Massingham 19 July 1943	Lt Col H. de Rancourt	Boston IIIA
Hunsdon 31 December 1943	Wg Cdr A.G. Wilson	Ventura Mosquito FB VI 8/43
Hunsdon 31 December 1943	Wg Cdr H.J.W. Meakin DFC	Ventura Mosquito FB VI 8/43
Hunsdon 31 December 1943	Wg Cdr North DFC, AFC	Ventura Mosquito FB VI 9/43
Oulton 16 May 1944	Wg Cdr Des McGlinn	Stirling I III Fortress II 1/44
Oulton 16 May 1944	Capt. George E. Paris to 4/44 Lt Col Clayton A. Scott	B-17F B-17G
Oulton 16 May 1944		Fortress I, II, III

APPENDIX IV

AIRCRAFT LOSSES 1943

Date	Crew	Aircraft
22/05/1943	Lt Le Bivic S/Lt Jacouinot Sgt-Chef L. Cohen Cpl-Chef Desertiaux	Boston IIIA AL285
22/05/1943	S/Lt Pineau	Boston IIIA BZ366
09/10/1943	Flt Lt Winston Smith (pilot) Fg Off. C.G. Macdonald	Mosquito VI HP850
09/10/1943	Sqn Ldr W.F. Wallington	Mosquito VI HX938
09/10/1943	Flt Lt E.W. Court	Mosquito VI HX937
09/10/1943	Flt Lt P.C. Kerr (pilot) Fg Off. B.J.E. Hannah	Mosquito VI HX912
22/10/1943		Mosquito VI HX948
23/10/1943		Mosquito VI HX956
23/10/1943		Mosquito VI HX831
24/11/1943	Flt Sgt N.A. Deakin (pilot) Flt Sgt T.J. Wesker	Mosquito VI HX978
27/11/1943	Fg Off. T.J.B. Shearer (pilot) Fg Off. R.J.T. Stirling	Mosquito VI
29/11/1943	Fg Off. Barry (pilot) Flt Sgt Walsh	Mosquito VI
30/11/1943		Mosquito VI HX983

Location	Squadron	Comments
Near Rougham, Norfolk	342 (Lorraine)	All crew killed after accident in low-level training.
Langerbrugge, Belgium	342 (Lorraine)	Failed to return from low-level attack.
Attack on aero engine works, Woippy, nr Metz	464	Crew missing.
Woippy raid	487	Willebrouck area.
Woippy raid	487	Antwerp area.
Woippy raid	464	Crew killed.
Sculthorpe: overshot landing	464	
Sculthorpe: overshot landing	21	
Sculthorpe: overshot landing	487	
Crash 1 mile N. of Newborough, Northants.	21	Both crew killed.
Attack on targets in NW Germany.	21	Crew missing
Crashed in sea after attacking airfields N. France (a/c on attachment at Ford).	464	Both crew killed.
Crash Coxford Heath after engine failed.	464	

Date	Crew	Aircraft
01/12/1943	Sqn Ldr A.S. Cussens (pilot) Fg Off. H.M. Mackay (Nav.)	Mosquito VI HX962
10/12/1943	Fg Off. M.L.B. Frankson (pilot) Plt Off. D.E. Cake (Nav.)	Mosquito VI HX966
10/12/1943	Flt Sgt T. Mair (pilot) WO K. Blow (Nav.)	Mosquito VI HX975

Location	Squadron	Comments
Anti-ship attack operating out of Predannack. Crashed in sea off Ile de Groix, Brittany.	487	Cussens missing. Mackay buried in Guidel Communal Cem.
Lost in attack on targets, NW Germany.	487	Crew buried at Emmen (Nieuw Dordrecht) Cem., Netherlands.
Lost in attack on targets, NW Germany.	487	Crew buried in Den Ham General Cem., Netherlands.

APPENDIX V

UNITS FROM 1949

Unit	Command	From
92nd Bomb Group (BG), Medium (comprising 325th, 326th & 327th Bomb Sqns) *First US unit post-war to operate from here.*	Strategic Air Command (SAC)	Spokane Army Airfield, Washington State (later AFB/ Fairchild AFB) 7 Feb. 1949 (det.)
98th Bomb Wing (BW), Medium (comprising 343rd, 344th & 345th Bomb Sqns)	SAC	Spokane Army Airfield (later AFB/Fairchild AFB). 15 May 1949 (det.)
63rd Bomb Sqn (BS), 43rd Bomb Group (BG)	SAC	Davis-Monthan Field (later AFB), Arizona 15 Aug. 1949 (det.)
19th Bomb Sqn (BS), Medium, 22nd Bomb Group (BG), Medium	SAC	March AFB, California Nov. 1949
23rd Strategic Reconnaissance Sqn (SRS) (Photographic) (5th SRG)	SAC	Fairfield-Suisun AFB (later Travis AFB), California. 22 Dec. 1949
49th Bomb Sqn, Medium, 2nd Bomb Group	SAC	Chatham AFB, Georgia 20 Feb. 1950 (det.)
301st Bomb Group, Medium, 352nd Bomb Sqn 353rd Bomb Sqn	SAC	Barksdale AFB, Louisiana (Home Base). RAF Scampton (det.) 17 May 1950 (also det.)
7502 Base Complement Sqn (later Air Support Wing)		April 1949
72nd Strategic Reconnaissance Sqn (Heavy), 5th Strategic Reconn. Wing (SRW)	SAC	Fairfield-Suisun AFB (later Travis AFB), California. 31 May 1950 (det.)

To	Commanding Officer	Aircraft
Spokane, April 1949	Col Salvatore E. Manzo	B-29
Spokane, 15 Aug. 1949 (90 day TDY)	Col Richard D. Dick	B-29
Tucson, Arizona 15 Nov. 1949	Lt Col Ralph W. Stanley	KB-29M tanker B-50A
Feb. 1950	Lt Col Lloyd D. Chapman	B-29
6 March 1950	Lt Col Fitzhugh Whitfield	RB-29
20 May 1950	Lt Col George L. Newton, Jr.	B-29 B-50A KB-29M
Lakenheath 11 July	Col Harris E. Rogner (Gp commander) Lt Col Donald G. McPherson (352nd BG) Maj. D. Richards (353rd BG)	B-29 KB-50M
May 1951	Lt Col Franklin M. Cochrane Jr. to 2/50. Maj. Richard A. Bosworth (temp.) Lt Col Charles Wimberly from 6/50. Col Thomas G. Corhin	C-47
July to Marham, later Burtonwood. 15 Nov. 1950 to Andersen AFB, Guam.	Lt Col Martin B. Schofield	RB-29

Unit	Command	From
97th Bomb Wing HQ, Medium, 97th Bomb Group (comprising 340th , 341st & 342nd Bomb Sqns)	SAC	Biggs AFB, Texas 15–17 July 1950 (det.) Also dets to Wyton and Waddington.
91st Strategic Reconnaissance Wing (SRW) – *first permanent unit on handover to USAF.* RAF Special Duty Flt	SAC	Lockbourne AFB, Ohio. Various detachments: 19 Jan. 1951
50th Radio Controlled Airplane Target (det.)		June 1951
3911 Air Base Group	SAC	16 May 1951
9th Air Rescue Sqn (ARS)		Manston Aug./Sept. 1951 (also at Burtonwood)
19th Bomb Sqn, 22nd Bomb Wing – *the last SAC bomber deployment.*	SAC	March AFB, California Sept 1951 (det.) (to Mildenhall)
1st Tactical Support Sqn	Tactical Air Command (TAC)	Langley AFB, Virginia 14 April 1952
49th Air Division HQ. Provided transport & communications support for USAF tactical forces in UK.	TAC	1 June 1952
38th Strategic Reconnaissance Sqn (SRW), Medium		Ramey AFB, Puerto Rico 5 April 1952 (det.)
60th Troop Carrier Wing (TCW)		May 1952
47th Bomb Wing (BW), Light (47th Bomb Wing, Tactical from 1 Oct. 1955)	TAC	Langley AFB, Virginia 1 June 1952

To	Commanding Officer	Aircraft
Aug. 1950 341st BS to Valley, 342nd to Waddington. Departed 9 Feb. 1951.	Brig. Gen. D.W. Hutchinson (97th BW) Col Dalene E. Bailey (97th BG) to 1/51. Col Harvey C. Dorney to 2/51. Lt Col H.E. Hunfield (341st BS) Maj. P. Beard (342nd BS) Lt Col Mills (340th BS)	B-50D
Lockbourne AFB, Ohio. Dec. 1952 Also det. to Japan.	Jan. to Aug. 1951: Col Horace M. Wade Col Landon E. McConnell Col Lewis E. Lyle Col Henry K. Mooney Col Joseph J. Preston to 1/53	RB-45C KB-29P
June 1955		OQ-19D drone
5 June 1952		
Nov. 1952 (approx.)		SB-29 Grumman SA-16A Albatross
Nov. 1951	Col James V. Edmundsen	B-29
Redesignated 1st Tactical Depot Sqn (TDS) June 1954. Det. 3 at Sculthorpe.	Lt Col Carl L. Killian (1953)	
1 July 1956	Col James D. Jones to 2/52 Brig. Gen. John D. Stevenson to 2/55 Brig. Gen. James F. Whisenand to 1/56	L-20A T-33A C-119 C-47
RAF Upper Heyford 9 Aug. 1952 (det.)	Maj. Lee R. Williams, Jr.	RB-50
Dec. 1954		C-119 L-20
Laughlin AFB, Texas 22 June 1962	Col David M. Jones Col John G. Glover Brig. Gen. Joseph R. Holzapple Col Reginald J. Clizbe Col Kenneth C. Dempster Col George H. Kneen, Jr.	B-45 1951–58 B-26 1951–52 RB-45 1954–56 B-66 1958–62 KB-50 1960–62

Unit	Command	From
84th Bomb Sqn, Light, 47th Bomb Wing	TAC	Langley AFB 31 May 1952
85th Bomb Sqn, Light (later Tactical), 47th Bomb Wing	TAC	Langley AFB 31 May 1952
422nd Bomb Sqn (later renumbered 86th BS)	TAC	20 Dec. 1953
86th Bomb Sqn, Light, 47th Bomb Wing	TAC	Activated 23 March 1954 at Sculthorpe (from 422nd BS). Returned to Sculthorpe 5 Aug. 1959
19th Tactical Reconnaissance Sqn (TRS), 47th Bomb Wing (Night Photo)	TAC Reassigned from 3rd Air Force to 12th Air Force 1 Dec 1956. Later att. to 66th TRW 12/57 & 10th TRW from 1/58	Shaw AFB, South Carolina 11 May 1954
9th Aviation Field Depot Squadron (AFDS)		Sandia, New Mexico 22 March 1953
67th Air Rescue Sqn (ARS)		Constituted 14 Nov. 1952

To	Commanding Officer	Aircraft
22 June 1962	Lt Col George B. Thabault Lt Col Raymond L. Fitzgerald (1953) Col Marshall R. Peterson, Jr. (1955) Maj. William P. Baker, Jr. (1957) Lt Col J. Morrow Maj. Donald H. Orr (1962)	B-45A B-66B 1/58
Laughlin AFB, Texas 22 June 1962	Lt Col Hubert M. Blair to 3/53 Lt Col George B. Leaverton to 12/54 Maj. Robert E. Grovert to 7/55 Maj. Keith Conley to 12/57 Maj. Carl L. Pacharzina, Jr. To 8/58 Lt Col Jack C. West to 2/61 Lt Col William L. Sheppard to 6/62	B-45 B-66B 1/58
Alconbury 15 Sept 1955 Inactivated 22 June 1962.	Lt Col Edward M. Miller to 5/55 Lt Col Robert E. Adamina to 6/57 Maj. Francis R. Riggs to 3/58 Lt Col Raymond A. Fulton to 6/61 Maj. William A. Nolte, Jr. to 1/62 Maj. Charles M. Sargen to 6/62	RB-45C 1954–58 B-66 1958–62
Spangdahlem, Germany. 10 Jan. 1959	Maj. John B. Anderson to 8/57 Maj. Everett G. Walker to 8/58 Maj. Robert L. Hopkins (temp.) to 10/58 Lt Col LeWis J. Partridge to 2/62	RB-45C RB-66 1/57
Inactivated 8 July 1954 – personnel reassigned to 1st Tactical Depot Sqn (TDS). Det. 3 at Sculthorpe.	Col Andrew L. Cox (1955) Lt Col Charles C. Malitz, Jr. (1957)	
Prestwick 4 Nov. 1953	Capt. Gerald E. Weatherman to 3/53 Lt Col Edward C. Lass	SA-16A SB-29 C-82A C-47

Unit	Command	From
7554th Target (8554) Towing Flt (TTF) – became 5th Target Tow Sqn, 25 June 1954.	Became det. of 5th TTS	Bentwaters 16 Dec. 1952 to Fürstenfeldbruck, Germany to Neubiberg 16 July 1954 det. to Sculthorpe.
47th Bomb Group Support Sqn		1954
47th Ordnance Survey (OS)		Dec. 1954
55th Fighter–Bomber Sqn (FBS), 20th Fighter–Bomber Wing (FBW)		Wethersfield 9 Aug. 1955
420th Air Refuelling Sqn (ARS)	TAC	Alexandria (later England) AFB, Louisiana. 9 Oct. 1955
78th Fighter–Bomber Sqn (FBS)		Shepherds Grove, Suffolk. 31 May 1956
Sculthorpe Base Flt		Feb. 1958
34th Bomb Sqn, Tactical	SAC	Eglin AFB, Florida. 18 Jan. to 4 March 1958
7375 Support Group		July 1962
28th Weather Reconnaissance Sqn (WRS)		HQ South Ruislip 1949. HQ Bushy Park March 1951. To RAF Northolt Oct 1962. Dets at Sculthorpe during 1950s onwards.
39th Antiaircraft Artillery (AAA) Battalion	US Army	Feb. 1951
172nd Chemical Smoke Company		
Aero Club		June 1963
7519th Combat Support Sqn, 48th Tactical Fighter Wing (TFW)		April 1967 – *USAF designated airfield as Dispersed Operating Base.*

To	Commanding Officer	Aircraft
Dets until 1957	Capt. Joe Campbell (1955)	TB-26 Invader L-5 Sentinel
Feb. 1958		C-119G L-20
Feb. 1958		
Wethersfield 27 April 1956	Maj. John J. Kropenick	F-84
Edwards AFB, California. 25 March 1964	Maj. James B. Young to 12/55 Lt Col James R. Sheffield to 1/59 Lt Col Henry A. Dafler to 1/60 Maj. Clyde G. Miller to 3/60 Lt Col Theodore J. Tanner to 6/61 Lt Col Lawrence E. Spears to 8/63 Lt Col Joseph F. McAllister to 3/64	KB-29P (to 2/58) KB-50 (1/57-) KB-50J (2/58-)
Shepherds Grove 3 May 1957	Maj. Robert R. Fredette to 12/56 Maj. Herbert O. Brennan	F-84F
22 Feb. 1962		T-33 T-29A C-47
Eglin		B-66
1 June 1964		
	Lt Col John J. Allen (1953) Lt Col Arnold R. Hull (1955)	WB-50D
US Army units left in 1957	Lt Col Nyles W. Baltzer (1951) Lt Col Peter J. Lacey (1951) Lt Col Frank D. Pryor, Jr. (1953)	
	Capt. Richard A. Houser	
March 1964		Aeronca &AC, 11AC
Disbanded 1976	Lt Col Alfred Bowman	

Unit	Command	From
457th Tactical Fighter Sqn (TFS), Air Force Reserve (USAF) (det.) (code SH)		10 June 1978
No. 55 Sqn (det.) No. 57 Sqn (det.) No. 100 Sqn (det.)	Royal Air Force	RAF Marham July 1978
231 OCU (det.) 232 OCU (det.)	Royal Air Force	RAF Marham July 1978
No. 6 Sqn (det.) No. 41 Sqn (det.) No. 54 Sqn (det.)	Royal Air Force	RAF Coltishall 14 June 1982
112 Tactical Fighter Sqn (det.) 162 TFS (det.) 166 TFS (det.) (code OH)	Ohio Air National Guard (ANG)	5 April 1983
492, 493, 494, 495 Tactical Fighter Sqns, 48th Tactical Fighter Wing (det.) (code LN)		Lakenheath since 15 Jan. 1960 6 June 1983 (det.) Also 1985.
480 Tactical Fighter Sqn, 52nd Tactical Fighter Wing. (det.) (code SP)		2 July 1984
23 TFS, 52nd TFW 81 TFS, 52nd TFW		1–19 Aug. 1984 19 Aug.–7 June 1984
112, 162, 166 Tactical Fighter Sqns (code OH)	Ohio ANG	7 June 1986
317 Tactical Airlift Wing		June 1988
463 Tactical Airlift Wing		Aug. 1988
772 Tactical Airlift Sqn, 313 Tactical Airlift Group		Aug. 1988
317 Tactical Airlift Wing		Oct. 1988
17 Reconnaissance Wing		April 1989
112 TFS 162 TFS (code OH)	Ohio ANG	21 May 1989

To	Commanding Officer	Aircraft
23 June 1978	Lt Col Leo J. Canavan	F-105D
May 1979		Victor K2 Victor K2 Canberra B2, E15, T4, T19.
May 1979		Canberra T4 Victor K2
16 Dec. 1982		Jaguar GR1
16 April 1983		A-7K
4 Aug. 1983		F-111F
		F-4E, F-4G
		F-4E, G
19 June 1986		A-7D, K
Aug. 1988		C-130E
Sept. 1988		C-130E
Oct. 1988	Lt Col Robert H. Meyers	
Dec. 1988		C-130E
15 Nov. 1989		TR-1A, B
17 June 1989		A-7D, K

APPENDIX VI

SUPPORT UNITS AND COMMANDING OFFICERS IN 1953, 1955 AND 1957

Unit	1953
HQ 47th Maintenance and Supply Group (later HQ 47th Support Group)	Col Ward W. Martindale
47th Field Maintenance Squadron	Maj. Dana W. Stewart
47th Supply Squadron	Maj. Jahnke E. Ernst
HQ Squadron Section 47th Air Base Group	Lt Col James S. Kale
47th Air Base Squadron	
47th Operations Squadron	
3rd Communications Squadron	Capt. John Elchak, Jr.
47th Communications Squadron	Capt. Hubert Green Capt. Harry P. Jones
47th Air Police Squadron	Maj. William V. Davies
47th Motor Vehicle Squadron (later 47th Transportation Squadron)	Capt. Albert L. Neyhard
47th Installations Squadron	Maj. Julian E. Perkinson
47th Food Service Squadron	Capt. Nathan J. James
47th Tactical Hospital	Maj. Benjamin H. Hammers (47th Medical Gp commander)
7565th USAF Hospital	
B-45 Mobile Training Detachment	

1955	1957
Col Leon L. Lowry	Col Leon L. Lowry
Maj. Warren T. Whitmire	Maj. Nelson A. Gerber
Lt Col Daniel B. Lockman	Maj. Granville E. Greene
Col John F. Harris	
	Maj. James K. Holmes
	Maj. Ben D. Newsom
Capt. George H. Anderson, Jr.	
Maj. John D. Ford, Jr.	Maj. Frederic E. Mau
Maj. William A. Banks	Maj. William A. Banks
Maj. Howard F. Bolton	
Maj. James K. Holmes	
Maj. Jack M. Gilliland	Maj. Hugh B. McManus, Jr
Lt Col Robert M. Coombs	
Maj. John M. Hegewald	

Unit	1953
HQ 49th Air Division (*see also* Units from 1949)	Col George B. Thabault (Director of Operations)
603rd Communications Squadron	
605th Communications Squadron	
28th Weather Squadron Detachment	Lt Col John J. Allen
Detachment 28-2, 28th Weather Squadron	
Detachment 28-5, 28th Weather Squadron	
1979-1 AACS (Airways and Air Communications Detachment)	1st Lt John C. Patrick
1245th AACS Squadron	
125th AACS	
604th ACWRON (Aircraft Control & Warning Squadron), Det. 5 (A C & W Sqn)	1st Lt Robert S. Pittsenbargar
7560th Air Base Squadron	
7560th Air Police Squadron	
7560th USAF Dispensary	
7560th Material Squadron (USAFE)	
Detachment 4 3rd Air Postal Squadron	

1955	1957
Col Robert E. Greer (Director of Operations)	
Maj. James Stotts	
	Maj. Kenneth E. George
Lt Col Arnold R. Hull	
	Maj. Harold E. Ivey
Maj. James G. Hall, Jr.	
	Maj. John H. Hockensmith
Capt. Frank C. Steinke	
Col James Baker (Base Commander) Lt Col Robert Neal (Squadron Commander)	
Capt. John F. Reynolds	
Capt. Kenneth A. Altman (Base Surgeon)	
Maj. Robert C. Reeve	
	Lt Lemuel N. John, Jr.

APPENDIX VII

AIRCRAFT LOSSES FROM 1949

Date	Pilot	Aircraft	Station
06/04/49	William H. Eckles	B-29 44-62111	Spokane, Washington
06/06/49		B-29 42-65353	Sculthorpe
25/06/49	Karl C. Ascherfeld	B-29 44-69977	Sculthorpe
21/07/49	Thomas F. Eastiman	B-29A 44-62141	Sculthorpe
07/06/50	Henry J. Walsh	B-29A 42-94081	Fairfield–Suisun AAF, California
15/11/50	William S. Chandler	B-50D 49-277	Sculthorpe
10/01/51	Lester C. Hess	B-50D 49-296	Biggs AFB, Texas
04/03/51	None – aircraft parked.	C-47A 42-23356	Sculthorpe
26/03/51	Arthur G. Preacher	KB-29P 44-86249	Sculthorpe
15/05/51	Robert J. Lyells	RB-45C 49-026	Sculthorpe
06/06/51	Eugene V. Brommelsiek	RB-45C 48-027	Barksdale AFB, Louisiana
07/06/51	Charles S. Graham	RB-45C 48-021	Barksdale AFB, Louisiana

Location	Sqn	Gp/Wg	Comments
Sculthorpe	325	92	Aircraft wrecked.
Sculthorpe	343	98	Fire on ground. Aircraft damaged.
Sculthorpe	343	98	Engine damaged.
Wisbech, Cambs	344	98	Aircraft wrecked. Caught fire in-flight. Abandoned in-flight.
North Sea (20 miles E. of Cromer)	72	5	Caught fire in-flight after gun turret fired into engine. 7 crew died.
Montpellier, France	342	97	Engine failure. Crew parachuted to safety.
Sculthorpe	340	97	
Neubiberg AB, Germany	HQ SQN	7502	Aircraft damaged in ground accident.
Sculthorpe	91	91 SRG	Take-off accident.
Sculthorpe	323 SRS	91 SRG	Damaged on landing.
Sculthorpe	323	91	
Sculthorpe	323	91	

Date	Pilot	Aircraft	Station
08/07/51	Don J. Weir	C-47A 42-23356	Sculthorpe
12/09/51	Louis L. Pfeffer	RB-45C 48-020	Lockbourne AFB, Ohio
21/09/51	Virgil R. Broyhill	SB-29 42-63750	Sculthorpe
05/10/51	Robert M. Horsky	B-29 44-27278	Sculthorpe
20/10/51	Robert H. Ahlborn	RB-45C 48-040	Lockbourne AFB, Ohio
24/10/51	Curtis G. Wyrtzen	B-45A 47-052	Sculthorpe
18/03/52	Henry J. Rodgers	B-45A 47-043	Sculthorpe
24/04/52	Elmer C. Keppler	B-50E 47-127	Sculthorpe
03/08/52	Bernard W. Watts	B-45A 47-083	Sculthorpe
07/11/52		C-47A 42-38100	Sculthorpe
07/11/52	Gordon D. Cramer	RB-45C 48-036	Sculthorpe
14/12/52	Louis A. Goelby	B-45A 47-070	Sculthorpe
07/03/53	William B. Owens	T-33A 51-6648	Sculthorpe
09/03/53	John H. Mykicz	B-45A 47-078	Sculthorpe
02/04/53	Zacheus W. Ryall, Jr.	B-45A 47-079	Sculthorpe
21/04/53	Zacheus W. Ryall, Jr.	B-45A 47-068	Sculthorpe
11/05/53	Robert F. Maloney	B-45A 47-080	Sculthorpe
13/05/53	Albert A. Weems	B-45A 47-066	Sculthorpe

Location	Sqn	Gp/Wg	Comments
Gand, Belgium	HQ SQN	3911	Weather related accident.
Sculthorpe	324	91	
Sculthorpe	9 ARS		Take-off accident due to mechanical failure.
Sculthorpe	2	22	Landing accident due to weather.
Sculthorpe	324	91	
Sculthorpe	324	91 SRG	Take-off accident due to mechanical failure.
Sculthorpe	322	91 SRW	Mechanical failure.
Sculthorpe	4	55	
Sculthorpe	84	47	Aircraft damaged on landing. Structural failure.
Sculthorpe	47	47	
Sculthorpe	4	91	
Fürstenfeldbruck, Germany	85	47	Aircraft shed both wings. Pilot killed while bailing out.
Sculthorpe	84	47	Crashed in belly landing.
8 miles S of Cambridge	85	47	Accident due to fire.
20 miles ENE of Cromer	85	47	Engine failure/engine fire.
Sculthorpe	85	47	Engine failure/engine fire.
20 miles E of Cromer	84	47	Engine failure/engine fire.
Sculthorpe	85	47	Engine failure/engine fire.

Date	Pilot	Aircraft	Station
26/05/53	George D. Hoffman	C-119C 50-121	Neubiberg AB, Germany
20/06/53	George B. Thabault	F-84G 51-927	Bentwaters
01/07/53	Bruno M. Larsen	B-45A 47-072	Sculthorpe
19/07/53	Robert E. Grovert	B-45A 47-069	Sculthorpe
10/09/53	Doy Baxter	T-33A 51-6645	Sculthorpe
08/10/53	Louis B. Panther	B-45A 47-039	Sculthorpe
27/11/53	None – aircraft parked.	C-47D 43-49360	Sculthorpe
14/12/53	Wilfred N. Ridenour	B-29 44-86308	Sculthorpe
09/01/54	John H. Cronin, Jr	B-45A 47-073	Sculthorpe
04/03/54	Hubert M. Blair	B-45A 47-062	Sculthorpe
08/04/54	Charles E. Sala	B-45A 47-077	Sculthorpe
23/04/54	Charles E. Sala	B-45A 47-045	Sculthorpe
29/04/54	Donald F. Orr	B-45A 47-067	Sculthorpe
04/06/54	Walter K. Padbury	B-45A 47-094	Sculthorpe
09/06/54	Theodore J. Leibrock	B-45A 47-061	Sculthorpe
18/06/54	Raymond L. Fitzgerald	B-45A 47-059	Sculthorpe
12/07/54	Galen B. Price	B-45A 47-071	Sculthorpe
31/08/54	Edward J. Sanderson	B-45A 47-056	Sculthorpe

Location	Sqn	Gp/Wg	Comments
Sculthorpe	40	317	
Sculthorpe	79 FBS	20 FBG	Forced landing due to engine failure/fire.
22 miles SSW of Rhein-Main AB, Germany	85	47	Weather related accident.
100 miles SSW of Sculthorpe.	85	47	Structural failure.
Sculthorpe	85	47	Landing accident.
Norton AFB, California	84	47	Crew killed – after aircraft in stall/spin.
Lisbon, Portugal		47	Ground accident.
Prestwick, Scotland	67 ARS	9 ARG	Aircraft wrecked in forced landing.
RAF Watton	85		Taxiing accident.
Rhein-Main AB, Germany	422	47	Aircraft damaged in take-off accident.
Sculthorpe	85	47	Ground accident caused by explosion.
5 miles SSW of Sculthorpe	86	47	Structural failure.
25 miles S of London	85	47	Structural failure.
Sculthorpe	85	47	Ground accident, explosion and fire.
Sculthorpe	84	45	Ground accident and explosion.
Argentia, Newfoundland	84	47	Landing accident.
51-50W 01-30E, UK	85	47	
Sculthorpe	86	47	Take-off accident.

Date	Pilot	Aircraft	Station
09/10/54	Warren R. Lewis	T-33A 52-9863	Sculthorpe
06/12/54	Jarold B. Wellen	F-84G 51-933	Woodbridge
11/12/54	James T. Leibrock	B-45A 47-073	Sculthorpe
11/01/55	John Bacon, Jr.	T-33A 51-6628	Sculthorpe
31/01/55	James W. Hood	T-33A 53-5048	Sculthorpe
28/02/55	Alan R. Morgan	L20A 52-6132	Sculthorpe
31/03/55	Bernard W. Watts	B-45A 47-042	Sculthorpe
19/04/55	Norman J. Powler, Jr.	B-45A 47-092	Sculthorpe
30/07/55	Marvin Hamilton	B-45A 47-058	Sculthorpe
25/10/55	Fred G. Jones	F-84F 52-6668	Sculthorpe
10/11/55	Clent Houston	F-84F 52-6665	Sculthorpe
09/12/55	Roy G. Evans	F-84F 52-6692	Sculthorpe
30/01/56	Capt. George W. Duncan (pilot), Capt. John Murray (co-pilot), 1st Lt John O'Mahoney	B-45A 47-059	Sculthorpe
14/03/56	Keith Conley	B-45A 47-072	Sculthorpe
05/12/56	1st Lt John Rossman Tinklepaugh (pilot), 1st Lt Guy Waller (passenger)	L-20A Beaver 52-6145	Bentwaters/ Woodbridge
03/06/57	Edwin L. Phillips	B-45A 47-071	Sculthorpe
02/07/57		KB-50J 48-0046	

Location	Sqn	Gp/Wg	Comments
West Barsham			Aircraft wrecked after flameout.
Sculthorpe	79	20	Aircraft wrecked.
Billy Mitchell Field, Milwaukee, Wisconsin	84	47	Landing accident.
Neubiberg, Germany	84	47	Landing accident causing ground loop.
Sculthorpe	85	47	
Sculthorpe		47	
Sculthorpe	86	47	Crash landing owing to mechanical failure.
Sculthorpe	84	47	
Sculthorpe	86		Taxiing accident due to mechanical failure.
30 miles S of Nouasseur AB, French Morocco	55 FBS		Aircraft wrecked after flameout. Pilot parachuted to safety.
Nouasseur AB, French Morocco	55		Landing accident.
Lodge Moor, Sheffield	55		Aircraft wrecked. Pilot survived.
3 miles E of Brandon	84	47	Aircraft was attempting to land at Lakenheath. All three crew killed.
Sculthorpe	85	47	
Bramah Edge, Peak District		81 FBW	A/c flying from Sculthorpe to Burtonwood so passenger (a pilot) could pick up an F-84 which had been at B'wood for maintenance and fly it back to Sculthorpe. Both crew killed.
1 mile ESE of Field Dalling, Norfolk	85	47	
Sculthorpe	420 ARS		Ground fire.

Date	Pilot	Aircraft	Station
20/09/57	Torino V. DiSalvo	B-45A 47-083	Sculthorpe
30/03/58	1st Lt W.H. Fulton Capt. G.T. Dugan A/1C E.W. Churchill	B-66B 55-0314	Sculthorpe
14/04/58	Capt. R.E. Taylor, 1st Lt R.B. Handcock, TSG B.M. Valencia	RB-66 54-0422	Sculthorpe
13/06/58	Airman 2nd Cl Mechanic Vernon L. Morgan	B-45A Tornado 47-046	Alconbury
03/07/58	Capt. William A. Marcum (pilot) 1st Lt C. Costen, Jr. Capt. W.B. Gray.	RB-66B 54-433A	Sculthorpe
16/03/61	Capt. H.V. Armani, 1st Lt F.W. Whitley, Jr., Capt. D. Harvey	RB-66 53-0430	Sculthorpe
26/10/61	Maj. P. Brooks, Capt. P.J. Savage, Capt. R. Davenport	B-66 54-0499	Sculthorpe

Location	Sqn	Gp/Wg	Comments
1 mile W of RAF West Raynham	84	47	
Sculthorpe	84	47	Aircraft damaged on landing overshoot. Crew escaped unhurt.
Sculthorpe	19 TRS	10 TRW	Crashed on approach to Sculthorpe near West Barsham Hall while making blind landing as part of training flight. Weather good. Jet operating under simulated blackout. All three crew killed (see *Times* report 15 Apr.).
Abbots Ripton, Wood Walton.	86	47	Unauthorised take-off. Crash blocked Edinburgh to King's Cross railway line.
Saxlingham Nethergate, Norfolk	19		3 crew ejected safely after hydraulic systems failure. A/c flew on until fuel ran out.
North Sea	19		All crew killed.
North Sea, 40 miles off Cromer/Sheringham	85		Cromer (Wells?) lifeboat launched to search for crew. All crew lost.

INDEX

Note: Page numbers in *italics* refer to illustrations. There may also be textual references on these pages.

If you enjoyed this book, you may also be interested in…

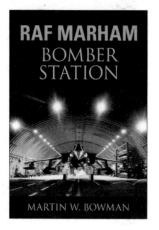

RAF Marham
MARTIN W. BOWMAN

RAF Marham's history reaches back into the First World War, when it aircraft served a vital home defence role, intercepting raiding Zeppelin and Gothas. In the late 1930s the station was reopened as a bomber base and, post-war, operated bombers and reconnaissance aircraft. It squadrons played a leading role in the Falklands and Gulf Wars, and over Bosnia and Iraq. Today the Marham Wing is one of the largest and busiest in the RAF, operating four squadrons of Tornado GR4 aircraft in the attack and reconnaissance roles.

9780752446943

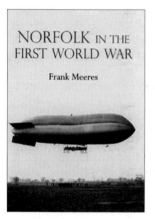

Norfolk in the First World War
FRANK MEERES

What was life like for Norfolk people during the First World War? This book sets out to answer that question, largely through contemporary sources: letters, diaries and journals, together with a wide range of visual material. From a look at life on the battlefronts to the home front, this book considers every aspect of the First World War for Norfolk: conscription conscientious objection, air raids, fear of invasion and the dangers of war to local fishermen. It describes how these dramatic events affected the lives of ordinary people, their patterns of work, diet and social behaviour. However, the main emphasis is on how men, women and children in the county lived, and died, during the four years of the Great War.

9781860772900

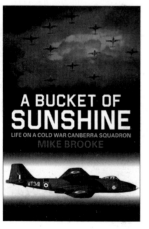

A Bucket of Sunshine
MIKE BROOKE

A Bucket of Sunshine – a term used for the deployment of a nuclear bomb – is a firsthand insight into life in the mid-1960s on a RAF Canberra nuclear-armed squadron in West Germany on the front line in the Cold War. Mike Brooke describes not only the technical aspect of the aircraft and its nuclear and conventional roles and weapons, but also majors on the low-level flying that went with the job of being ready to go to war at less than three minutes' notice. Brooke tells his story warts and all, with many amusing overtones, in what was an extremely serious business when the world was standing on the brink of nuclear conflict.

9780752470214

Visit our website and discover thousands of other History Press books.

www.thehistorypress.co.uk